The Best
LITTLE
Grammar Book
Ever!

The BEST Little Grammar Book *Ever!*

101 Ways to Impress With Your Writing and Speaking

Arlene Miller

bigwords101
Petaluma, California

bigwords101
P.O. Box 4483
Petaluma, CA 94955
www.bigwords101.com
bigwords101@yahoo.com

ISBN 978-0-9843316-0-4

Library of Congress Control Number 2009941187

To Jake and Shelley,
who are my everything and my greatest inspirations!

Contents

Chapter 3
The Basics: Punctuation and Capitalization 36

Chapter 4
Things Not to Use   52

Chapter 5
Confusing Things 64

Chapter 6
Some Grammar Issues   **82**

Chapter 7
Finishing Touches 98

Acknowledgments

I would like to thank the following people for their support and help in making this book a reality.

Edie Partridge, Dave Noderer, Patty Buzard, and Connie Peabody for their continuing support for this project.

John Lehmann for hiring me as an English teacher, where I have learned everything I ever wanted to know about grammar!

Joy Hermsen, without whose e-business course I never would have proceeded with this book.

Dan Poynter, Fern Reiss, Shel Horowitz, Aaron Shepard, and Michael Marcus for their books, which helped me learn so much about this publishing business.

Everyone at the Yahoo Self-Publishing Group, who provided so much useful information. Without this knowledge, I could never have completed this project.

Sheldon Siegel, K. Patrick McDonald, Myrna Ericksen, Dawn Josephson, Robin Kneeland, and Craig Guptill for their kind words.

Quoteland.com (www.quoteland.com) and The Quotations page (www.quotationspage.com) for the quotations.

Special thanks to my editors Ron Teplitz, Mary Jo Teplitz, and Carol Vuillmenot; and to my designer Marny Parkin and my cover designer Pete Masterson for their wonderful work.

Introduction

Okay. I admit it. Whenever I hear the word **I** used instead of **me,** or see the word **your** instead of **you're,** it is like hearing chalk squeaking across a blackboard! Years ago such grammatical mistakes wouldn't have bothered me, if indeed I noticed them at all. However, many years of writing, editing, and teaching English have polished up my skills and made me sensitive to such errors. During my years as a technical writer and editor, book editor, and now English teacher, I have seen the same errors, questions, and problems come up repeatedly. I decided to put these grammatical issues together in a book that would be different from the usual grammar book.

Although it does contain a review of grammar, this book is not a grammar textbook, nor is it a complete grammar reference. It is intended to address those issues that are most confusing to people when they write or speak. This book will be helpful to almost anyone who wants to write and speak (and even e-mail) correctly—students from junior high school through college; anyone looking for that first job, a better job, or a new career; career professionals; those whose native language is not English; and just about anyone else who has ever had a question related to grammar or writing.

How to Use This Book

The *Best Little Grammar Book Ever* contains both a grammar review (Chapters 1, 2, and 3) and common mistakes and problems in writing and speaking (Chapters 4, 5, 6, and 7). It is neither a complete grammar textbook nor a complete grammar reference; if it were, it would be called *The Best **Big** Grammar Book Ever!* I decided to focus on the topics that cause the most confusion, questions, and errors.

I recommend, therefore, that the best way to use this book is to first read through it. After you have read it and know what it contains, you can use it as a reference book to remind you of what you have learned. There is a short quiz at the beginning of each chapter with the answers on the following page. Take these fun quizzes to see how much you already know before you read the chapters!

The first three chapters of the book present a grammar review. Chapter 1 is all about the parts of speech. You probably learned them in grammar school, but maybe you have forgotten some of them. The parts of speech are the basic elements of the English language. Chapter 2 discusses sentence structure: What is the function of each word in a sentence? What is the difference between a sentence and a fragment? How can you write good sentences? What are phrases and clauses? Chapter 3 reviews capitalization and punctuation, those little symbols that allow you to understand the writing.

You do not need to memorize all the information contained in Chapters 1, 2, and 3. However, it is helpful to have an idea of what is contained in these chapters because the same concepts come up in the other chapters of the book. Do take time to learn any information that is contained in the **Helpful Hints,** which directly affect your writing and speaking.

Chapter 4 begins the discussion of common problems in grammar. In this chapter you will learn some things not to do in your writing and speaking. Chapter 5 talks about confusing words—those words that are similar but not the same—and tells you which is which. You will never again confuse **your** and **you're!** In Chapter 6 you will find a host of other common grammar issues including how to write possessives and how to write in a parallel structure. Chapter 7 contains the finishing touches: how to write numbers, how to write series and lists, the most commonly misspelled and mispronounced words, and, finally, how to write a paragraph and a multi-paragraph letter or essay.

You are holding this book. You are now on your way to becoming a more impressive writer and speaker. Take the quizzes, read on, and impress everyone with your knowledge of grammar!

If you have any comments on this book, or if you have a question about something that is not included here (and you think it should be), please contact me. I can be reached at bigwords101@ yahoo.com. Visit my Web-site at www.bigwords101.com.

Conventions Used in This Book

1. I have used **boldface** type for emphasis in examples and to indicate grammar vocabulary.

2. I have used **boldface italics** when I have used a word as itself, rather than as part of the sentence.

3. Notes are set off with dotted lines and contain important information.

4. Helpful Hints are set off with solid lines and contain information that will improve your writing and speaking.

5. I have used a conversational tone in this book to make it easy to read. In some cases you might notice I have done something I have told you to avoid in order to keep a casual tone and get my point across. These choices are stylistic and have nothing to do with correct grammar.

Chapter 1

The Basics:
Parts of Speech

Everything should be made as simple as possible,
but not one bit simpler.

Albert Einstein (attributed)
US (German-born) physicist (1879–1955)

1. Nouns   5. Adverbs
2. Pronouns   6. Prepositions
3. Verbs   7. Conjunctions
4. Adjectives   8. Interjections

You may remember hearing about the "parts of speech" way back in elementary school. The parts of speech are simply the categories into which every word in the language fits. These parts of speech are the building blocks of the English (or any) language. When people refer to the parts of speech, they mean the **eight** categories into which all words can be placed. I bet you remember terms such as *nouns* and *verbs,* but do you recall all eight parts of speech?

Let me mention two things before we continue:

1. Many words belong to more than one part of speech. It depends upon how the word is used in the sentence.

2. The world will not come to an end if you do not know the parts of speech. However, many times in this book, and in any grammar or writing book, the specific parts of speech will be referred to; after all, they are the building blocks upon which the language is built.

Here are the **eight** parts of speech:

1. Noun
2. Pronoun
3. Verb
4. Adjective
5. Adverb
6. Preposition
7. Conjunction
8. Interjection

This chapter briefly discusses these eight parts of speech. Read on . . .

Chapter 1 Quiz:
How Much Do You Know
About the Parts of Speech?

Take this quiz before you read Chapter 1. The answers are on the back of this page.

Match each word with its part of speech:

1. wow! _____   a. noun
2. bring _____   b. pronoun
3. purple _____   c. verb
4. beside _____   d. adjective
5. but _____   e. adverb
6. children _____   f. preposition
7. slowly _____   g. conjunction
8. he _____   h. interjection

9. Which of the following words is a proper noun? ___
   a. boys   b. them   c. family   d. Boston

Name two coordinating conjunctions besides **and:**

10. _____   11. _____

12. Which of these words is a collective noun? _____
   a. girls   b. family   c. people   d. James

13. Which of these words is a personal pronoun? _____
   a. me   b. animal   c. Paris   d. who

What parts of speech are **gave** and **to** in this sentence?
   I **gave** a book **to** him.
14. **gave?** _____   15. **to?** _____

Answers to Chapter 1 Quiz

1. wow!   h. interjection
2. bring   c. verb
3. purple   d. adjective
4. beside   f. preposition
5. but   g. conjunction
6. children   a. noun
7. slowly   e. adverb
8. he   b. pronoun

9. Which of the following words is a proper noun?
    a. boys   b. them   c. family   ***d. Boston***

10 and 11. Name two coordinating conjunctions besides ***and***:
    Any two of these are correct (one point for each one correct):
    but, so, for, or, nor, yet

12. Which of these words is a collective noun? ____
    a. girls   ***b. family***   c. people   d. James

13. Which of these words is a personal pronoun?
    a. me   b. animal   c. Paris   d. who

What parts of speech are ***gave*** and ***to*** in this sentence?
    I ***gave*** a book ***to*** him.
14. ***gave—verb***   15. ***to—preposition***

15 correct: Grammar Whiz!!
13–14 correct: Very Good!
11–12 correct: Pretty Good!
10 or fewer correct: Need Some Practice!

1. Nouns

Ah, think back to third grade. Does this sound familiar?

"A noun is a person, place, or thing."

A noun can also be an emotion or idea. Therefore, a noun is a person or thing of some type.

Here are some nouns:

sun	California	family
girl	doctor	religion
dog	book	Susie
happiness	rain	seashore

The words above are all people, places, things, ideas, or emotions.

People: Susie, girl, doctor, family
Places: California, seashore
Things: dog, book, sun, rain
Ideas or emotions: happiness, religion

Helpful Hint! How can you check to see if something is a noun? Usually, you can put the words **a, an,** or **the** before nouns.

Examples: the sun, a girl, a dog, a religion, the happiness

This often will not work with words that start with capital letters, such as California or Suzie. However, most words that start with capital letters are nouns anyway.

The Five Types of Nouns

There are five categories of nouns:

1. **Common nouns** are regular nouns that do not start with capital letters, such as **happiness, boy, desk,** and **city.**

2. **Proper nouns** are the nouns that start with a capital letter. They are specific people, places, things, or ideas such as **Florida, Buddhism, Joe,** and **Thanksgiving.**

3. **Concrete nouns** are nouns that represent things you can see, hear, smell, taste, or feel. Most nouns are concrete. Concrete nouns are either common or proper too. Concrete nouns include **grass, paper, perfume, air** (you can feel it), **Susie,** and **Golden Gate Bridge.**

4. **Abstract nouns** are the nouns that represent ideas or emotions; you cannot perceive them with your senses. **Religion, happiness, anger,** and **Buddhism** fall into this category.

5. **Collective nouns** are nouns that represent a group of things or people without being plural (although they can also be made plural). **Family, group, orchestra, audience, flock, bunch,** and **herd** fall into this category. These nouns become important when we discuss noun and verb agreement in Section 84 of this book.

2. Pronouns

A pronoun takes the place of a noun. For example, instead of saying

"Sally took Sally's books back to the library."

You say

"Sally took **her** books back to the library." **Her** is a pronoun. **Sally** is called the **antecedent.** (The antecedent is the word that the pronoun replaces.)

Some common pronouns are **I, you, he, she, them, they, we, us, him, her,** and **it.**

Helpful Hint! When you write, do not use a pronoun unless it is clear to what or whom it refers.

Types of Pronouns

There are six types of pronouns.

1. Personal pronouns are the common pronouns that are listed above, such as **I, me, you, he, she, it, they, her,** and **him.** They usually don't present any problem in writing unless the antecedent is unclear.

Example: I brought a hat, a scarf, and a coat, but *it* got lost. (What got lost?)

2. Demonstrative pronouns point things out. There are only four of them: *this, that, these,* and *those.*

Example: **This** is my new CD. (Once again, make sure you know what *this* refers to!)

3. Interrogative pronouns are used to ask questions. There are five of them: *which, who, whose, whom,* and *what.*

Example: **Who** is that man?

4. Relative pronouns begin adjective clauses (more about that later). There are five of them: *which, whom, whose, who,* and *that.* Notice that they are almost the same as the interrogative pronouns. However, relative pronouns do not ask a question, and they do not appear at the beginning of a sentence. Here are some examples of how they are used.

Examples: You can borrow the book **that** I just finished.

My neighbor, **who** is a lawyer, just came back from Paris.

5. Reflexive/intensive pronouns are the ones with *-self* at the end. Here are some examples:

Examples: I baked that cake **myself.** (reflexive—*myself* reflects back to *I*)

I **myself** baked that cake. (intensive—used to emphasize *I*)

Helpful Hint! Do not use the *-self* pronouns any other way. It is incorrect to say "He gave the book to **myself.**" It is correct to say, "He gave the book to **me.**" Never begin a sentence with a *-self* pronoun!

---

6. Indefinite pronouns include *someone, everyone, anyone, no one, somebody, anybody, everybody, everything, something, anything, nothing, none, few, many, several, all, some,* and many more. They are important because you need to know which ones are singular and which ones are plural, so you know which verb and personal pronoun to use with them.

Helpful Hint! *Someone, everyone, anyone, no one, everybody, nobody, anybody, somebody, something, everything, anything, nothing, each, either,* and *neither* are some common indefinite pronouns that are singular.

Example:	**Everyone is bringing his or her** own lunch to the picnic. (***Everyone*** is singular. The verb *is bringing* is singular, and the pronoun *his or her* is singular. They must all match.)
Example:	**Several are bringing their** own lunches to the picnic. (***Several*** is plural. The verb *are bringing* is plural, and the pronoun *they* is plural. They all match.)

How can you tell whether or not a verb is singular or plural? Use the verb with the pronoun *he* (which is singular), and whichever verb form you use is the singular form. Then, use the verb with the pronoun *they* (which is plural), and whichever verb form you use is the plural form.

Examples:	He *is walking* home. (*is walking* is the singular verb form.)
	They *are walking* home. (*are walking* is the plural verb form.)

Note: Do not confuse **pronouns** with **proper nouns.** Proper nouns begin with capital letters and are nouns (person, place, thing, idea). Pronouns are a separate part of speech.

Proper Nouns: New York, Henry, Buddhism, Italy, Red Cross

Pronouns: she, anyone, they, which

3. Verbs

Verb: It's what you do! Verbs are action words. ***Jump, run, bake, study, read, swim, give,*** and ***walk*** are examples of verbs.

Verbs can also indicate **mental** action, not just **physical** action. ***Think, wonder, plan,*** and ***consider*** are also verbs.

Examples: The boys **hid** in the forest. (***Hid*** is a verb.)

I **took** the math test yesterday. (***Took*** is a verb.)

The hotel **provided** us with rooms after the game. (***Provided*** is a verb.)

Helpful Hint! Every sentence needs a verb. Without a verb, there is no sentence!

Linking Verbs

There is another important type of verb called a **linking verb.** A linking verb ties together the word or words before the verb and the word or words after the verb. The linking verb is like the equal sign in math. The most common linking verb is the verb ***to be.*** That verb has many different forms. You probably recognize the ***to be*** verb by these familiar forms: ***is, am, are, will be, was, has been, have been,*** etc. Here are some linking verbs "in action":

Examples: I **am** hungry. (***Hungry*** describes ***I;*** they are linked by the verb ***am.***)

She ***was*** a dancer. (***Dancer*** describes ***she;*** they are linked by the verb ***was.***)

There are linking verbs other than the forms of the verb ***to be. Taste, appear, become,*** and ***feel*** are examples of linking verbs. Usually, if you can substitute a form of the ***to be*** verb and the sentence still makes sense, you have a linking verb.

Examples: She **felt** tired today. (***Tired*** describes ***she;*** they are linked by the verb ***felt. She is tired today*** makes sense.)

He ***became*** angry at me. (***Angry*** describes ***he***; they are linked by the verb ***became.*** **He <u>was</u> angry at me** makes sense.)

Mary **threw** the ball. (***Ball*** does not describe ***Mary***; ***threw*** is **not** a linking verb! **Mary <u>is</u> the ball** makes no sense.)

To make things just a bit more confusing, words like ***taste, smell,*** and ***feel*** are sometimes linking verbs and sometimes action verbs. Notice the difference:

Examples: The cake **tasted** great! (***Great*** describes ***cake***; ***tasted*** is a linking verb. The cake didn't do anything. There is no action here.)

I **tasted** the cake. (***Cake*** does not describe ***I***; ***taste*** is an action verb here.)

- -
Note: Why does it matter which verbs are linking and which are action? Good question! Sometimes it becomes important to know because it determines whether you use ***I*** or ***me***, ***him*** or ***he, she*** or ***her,*** etc. More about that later!
- -

Tenses

Verbs have some qualities you should know about. One of these is **tense,** which has to do with time. The tense of a verb tells you when the action took place. Verbs are the only action part of speech, and they can take place in the past, in the present, or in the future. There are 6 main tenses, each representing a different time. Each of the 6 has a partner (the **progressive** form), making the total number of tenses 12. Here they are, using the action verb ***walk***:

1. Present tense: I **walk** to the store. (It is happening now.)

   Present progressive tense: I **am walking** to the store.

2. Past tense: I **walked** to the store. (It happened in the past, and it is over.)

   Past progressive: I **was walking** to the store.

3. Future tense: I **will walk** to the store. (It will happen in the future. Please don't bother using **shall**.)

   Future progressive: I **will be walking** to the store.

4. Present perfect: I **have walked** to the store every day this week. (It happened in the past and is likely continuing.)

   Present perfect progressive: I **have been walking** to the store.

5. Past perfect: I **had walked** to the store before I met Sue. (It happened in the past by a certain time at which something else happened.)

   Past perfect progressive: I **had been walking** to the store when I met Sue.

6. Future perfect tense: I **will have walked** to the store by six o'clock. (It will happen in the future before some other future event.)

   Future perfect progressive: I **will have been walking** to the store every day this week by tomorrow.

Notice that the **progressive tenses** are the same, but the verb has the -**ing** ending.

Helpful Hint! You can probably figure out when to use the tenses. The important thing to remember is not to switch tenses without a reason. For example, "I **go** to the movies, and I **saw** my cousin there," is incorrect because the tense switches from present to past, when both things actually happened at the same time.

Note: Notice the words that are used with the verb **walk** in some of the tenses. Although they look like forms of the linking verb **to be,** they are not. Because they are with another verb (in this case, **walk**), they are called **helping verbs.** For example, in "I **will have been** walking," **will have been** are helping verbs, and **walking** is the main verb. If those words are used without a main verb, then they are linking verbs. For example, in "I **will have been** a teacher for three years," **will have been** is a linking verb. There is no other verb in the sentence, and **teacher** describes **I.** The verb and its helping verbs are called a **verb phrase.**

Here are the tenses for the verb *to be,* using the pronoun *you:*

Present/Present Progressive: you are/you are being

Past/Past Progressive: you were/you were being

Future/Future Progressive: you will be/you will be being

Present Perfect/Present Perfect Progressive: you have been/you have been being

Past Perfect/Past Perfect Progressive: you had been/you had been being

Future Perfect/Future Perfect Progressive: you will have been/you will have been being

- -

Note: Some verbs have irregular forms that you just have to memorize.

Examples: I **swam,** but I have **swum.**

She **drank,** but she has **drunk.**

I **bring,** but I have **brought** (not **brang** or **brung** or **broughten!**)

Refer to Section 91 for some common irregular verb forms.

- -

Voice

Another quality of verbs besides tense is **voice.** There are two voices: **active** and **passive**. In **active** voice, the **subject** of the sentence (usually, the noun or pronoun before the verb) is doing the action. Can you see the difference between the voices?

He **drove** to the mall. (**active**—the subject of the sentence, *he,* did the driving.)

He **was driven** to the mall by his sister. (**passive**)

Helpful Hint! When you write, use active voice most of the time. It is stronger and more effective.

Transitive/Intransitive

Oh, one more thing about verbs—yes, they are rather complicated! Verbs are also classified as either **transitive** or **intransitive**. The dictionary refers to verbs as either **vi** (verb intransitive) or **vt** (verb transitive) where it tells you the part of speech.

Transitive verbs have a direct object; intransitive verbs don't. Sometimes a verb can be both, depending on how it is being used in that particular instance. Direct objects are discussed in Section 11. Basically, if you ask **what** or **who** about the verb, the answer is the direct object. Here are some examples.

Example: They **played baseball.** (Played what? Baseball. ***Baseball*** is the direct object, and ***played*** is transitive.)

They **played** in the yard. (Played what or who? The sentence does not tell you. There is no direct object, and ***played*** is intransitive.)

Helpful Hint! Is it important to know if a verb is transitive or intransitive? Yes, sometimes, it is. There are some verbs that are confusing, and the one you use depends upon whether it is transitive or intransitive.

Example: He lies in the sun. (The verb is intransitive. Use ***lie.***)

He lays his hat on the table. (The verb is transitive. Use ***lay.***)

See Chapter 5 for more information about these confusing things!

Another Helpful Hint! You already learned in Section 1 that you can tell if a word is a noun by putting ***a, an,*** or ***the*** in front of it. How can you tell if a word is a verb? Put the word ***to*** in front of it. For example, to **jump,** to **think,** to **be,** to **study,** to **allow.**

4. Adjectives

Adjectives are pretty simple. They are used to describe nouns (people, places, things, ideas) and sometimes pronouns. Adjectives can also describe other adjectives. They tell **how many, what kind,** or **which ones.** Here are some examples of adjectives describing (or **modifying** nouns):

> **Pretty** bird, **six** trees, **blue** dress, **handsome** Harry, **good** idea

Here is an example of an adjective that describes a pronoun: He is **handsome.** Notice that the structure is a little different here. When describing a pronoun, the adjective is usually **after** the verb rather than right before the pronoun. Notice that the verb is **always** a linking verb (*is*, in this sentence) in this type of sentence.

Here is an adjective describing another adjective: **bright blue** dress. The adjective *blue* is describing the noun *dress.* However, the adjective *bright* is describing the type of *blue* (not the dress).

What if you said **new, blue** dress? *New* and *blue* are both adjectives, but they both describe the noun *dress.* It is a **new** dress, and it is a **blue** dress. It is not the **blue** that is **new**!

Helpful Hint! When both adjectives describe the noun (as in **new, blue** dress), make sure you put a comma between the two (or more) adjectives. When one adjective describes the other adjective (as in **bright blue** dress), do not use a comma.

Other Types of Adjectives

There are a couple of special types of adjectives. However, they have the same function as any other adjective.

1. Demonstrative: In Section 2 we discussed demonstrative pronouns. They are *this, that, these,* and *those.* These same four words, when placed right before a noun, are demonstrative adjectives. Notice the difference:

Examples: **This** is my book. (demonstrative pronoun)

                 This book is mine. (demonstrative adjective describing **book**)

2. Proper: Proper adjectives are just like proper nouns; they begin with a capital letter. Here are a few examples: **Thanksgiving** dinner, **Italian** food, **Catholic** religion.

Notes:

Some words can be used as more than one part of speech, depending on how they are used in that particular sentence. Nouns can often be used as adjectives. Here are some examples: beef stew, bread pudding, prom dress, Christmas vacation.

The words *a, an,* and *the* are called articles. Sometimes they are thought of as a separate part of speech, but they are really adjectives.

---

5. Adverbs

Like adjectives, adverbs are **describing words.** Adverbs are used to describe verbs (action words). Sometimes adverbs also describe adjectives or other adverbs. Adverbs tell **where, when,** and **how.** Adverbs usually end in *-ly,* but not always.

Examples: She ran *quickly*. *Quickly* describes how she *ran* (*ran* is the verb).

                 He is *extremely* intelligent. *Extremely* describes the adjective *intelligent*.

                 He writes *really* quickly. *Really* is an adverb that describes *quickly*, also an adverb. *Quickly* describes **how** he *writes (writes* is the verb).

Some words ending in *-ly* are adjectives, not adverbs, because they describe nouns. Here are some examples:

Examples: What a *lovely* dress. *Lovely* describes the noun *dress,* so it is an adjective.

I have three sisters, so I am never ***lonely. Lonely*** describes the pronoun ***I.*** The two words are linked with the linking verb ***am.*** (Note that the word ***never*** is an adverb telling **when.** It describes the adjective ***lonely.***)

Many adverbs do not end in ***-ly.*** Some of these adverbs include ***now, then, soon, very, only, often,*** and ***not.***

Helpful Hints!

1. There is usually more than one place to put an adverb in a sentence. Sometimes the location of an adverb changes the meaning of a sentence (for example, see Section 68 for a discussion about the adverb ***only.***) Other times, the sentence is simply clearer if you place the adverb close to the verb.

Example: I ***go*** for a walk in the woods ***often.***

I ***often go*** for a walk in the woods. (better way to write it)

2. Be careful not to overuse the adverbs ***really*** and ***very.*** Avoid using two ***really***'s or ***very***'s in a row! (for example, **really, really** cold!)

---

6. Prepositions

Prepositions are usually little words, and they are always part of a phrase (a group of a few related words) known, not surprisingly, as a **prepositional phrase.** A prepositional phrase generally consists of a **preposition,** sometimes an **article** (***a, an,*** or ***the***), and a **noun** or **pronoun** (which is called the **object of the preposition**). Prepositional phrases usually answer the questions where? or when?

Here are some examples of prepositions in a phrase (the preposition is in **bold**):

in the box	**down** the stairs
with my friends	**beside** the desk

at the store	**within** the city
out of the room	**for** the committee
of mine	**among** the students
between the books	**beneath** the table
by me	**after** the storm
to the movies	**before** his speech
up the tree	**along** the riverbank

There are other prepositions, but you get the idea!

If a preposition does not have a noun or pronoun after it, it is **not** a preposition; it is an adverb.

Example: I am going **inside the house** (prepositional phrase; *inside* is a preposition).

I am going **inside**. (There is no prepositional phrase. *Inside* is an adverb here.)

Helpful Hints! It is usually best not to end a sentence with a preposition.

Examples: Wrong: Where are you **at**?
Right: Where are you?

Wrong: Where are you going **to**?
Right: Where are you going?

Okay: Whom are you going **with**?
Better: With whom are you **going**?

It is important to be able to recognize prepositional phrases. Often, recognizing a prepositional phrase will help you decide whether to use *who* or *whom, I* or *me, him* or *he,* etc. We will talk about that in Section 58.

---

7. Conjunctions

Conjunctions are joining words. They join words, phrases (a short group of related words), or even sentences together. (See Section 12 for information about phrases.) The most common conjunction is **and.**

Examples: Jack **and** Jill (joins two words together)

I went to school **and** to the movies (joins two phrases together).

I am a student, **and** my brother is a dentist (joins two sentences).

And is called a **coordinating conjunction.** There are seven coordinating conjunctions in all. They are **for, and, nor, but, or, yet,** and **so.** The first letters of these words spell out **FANBOYS.**

Remember the "word" **FANBOYS** and you will remember these conjunctions!

Subordinating Conjunctions

The **FANBOYS** conjunctions are called **coordinating conjunctions** because they connect, or join, two or more things. There is another kind of conjunction, called a **subordinating conjunction.** These conjunctions begin **subordinate clauses** (See Section 13). Subordinating conjunctions include (but are not limited to) these words: **although, since, if, because, until, when,** and **whenever.**

Examples: **Although I am small**, I am strong (subordinate clause begins with **although**).

Because I have no money, I cannot go to the movies (subordinate clause begins with **because**).

I cannot get my license **until I turn sixteen** (subordinate clause begins with **until**).

Helpful Hints!

1. When you are joining two things, there is no comma. However, in a series or more than two things, it is generally preferable to use a comma before **and.**

Examples: I packed shoes and socks.

              I packed shoes, socks, and shirts.

2. There is generally a comma before a FANBOYS conjunction that connects two sentences.

Examples: I sprained my ankle, so I cannot go hiking today.

              I cannot go with you, but my sister can.

3. Avoid starting sentences with a FANBOYS conjunction. (Once again, they are **for, and, nor, but, or, yet, so.**)

---

8. Interjections

Wow! This is an easy one! Interjections are words that don't really grammatically belong to the sentence; they are usually exclamatory words but not always. Sometimes they are followed by an exclamation point; sometimes they are connected to the sentence by a comma.

Here are some interjections: **hey, gosh, ouch, gee whiz, wow, oh, well.**

Examples: **Wow!** What a nice car!

              Ouch! That really hurt!

              Well, I think I am going with you.

              Oh, I am sorry about that.

Chapter 2

The Basics:
Sentence Structure

Even if you do learn to speak correct English,
whom are you going to speak it to?

Clarence Darrow
US defense lawyer (1857–1938)

Words are combined to make up sentences. A sentence is a complete thought. Almost everything you read is made up of sentences. Every word in a sentence is, of course, one of the eight parts of speech. A sentence might contain more than one instance of a certain part of speech (for example, four nouns or three verbs or five adjectives) and does not need to contain all the parts of speech. In fact, hardly any sentence would contain all eight parts of speech. However, remember that each word in a sentence is one of the eight parts of speech. Each word in a sentence also performs a certain function in the sentence. These functions will be described in the following sections. The function a word performs in the sentence is not the same as its part of speech. **Parts of speech** refers only to these eight words: noun, pronoun, verb, adjective, adverb, preposition, conjunction, and interjection.

Chapter 2 Quiz:
How Much Do You Know
About Sentence Structure?

Take this quiz before you read Chapter 2. The answers are on the back of this page.

1. I gave Joe a computer for his birthday.
   The subject of this sentence is
   a. Joe   b. gave   c. birthday   d. I

2. The simple predicate of the sentence in #1 is
   a. Joe   b. gave   c. computer   d. I

3. The direct object of the sentence in #1 is
   a. computer   b. birthday   c. I   d. Joe

4. The indirect object of the sentence in #1 is
   a. computer   b. gave   c. I   d. Joe

5. What is the prepositional phrase in the sentence? _____

6. This is the television that I bought on sale.
   Underline the adjective clause in the sentence.

7. I cannot go on vacation because I have no money.
   Underline the adverb clause in the sentence.

8. I am.
   Is this a complete sentence?   a. Yes   b. No

9. Jack is a student, and his brother is a pilot.
   This sentence is
   a. simple   b. compound   c. complex   d. compound/complex

Answers to Chapter 2 Quiz

1. I gave Joe a computer for his birthday.
   The subject of this sentence is
   a. Joe   b. gave   c. birthday   **d. I**

2. The simple predicate of the sentence in #1 is
   a. Joe   **b. gave**   c. computer   d. I

3. The direct object of the sentence in #1 is
   a. computer   b. birthday   c. I   d. Joe

4. The indirect object of the sentence in #1 is
   a. computer   b. gave   c. I   **d. Joe**

5. What is the prepositional phrase in the sentence? **for his birthday**

6. This is the television **that I bought on sale.**
   Underline the adjective clause in the sentence.

7. I cannot go on vacation **because I have no money.**
   Underline the adverb clause in the sentence.

8. I am.
   Is this a complete sentence?   **a. yes** b. No

9. Jack is a student, and his brother is a pilot.
   This sentence is
   a. simple   **b. compound** c. complex d. compound/complex

9 correct: Grammar Whiz!!
7–8 correct: Very Good!
6 correct: Pretty Good!
5 or fewer correct: Need Some Practice!

9. Subjects

The subject of the sentence is **always** a noun or a pronoun, although it is not always a person. It is usually whatever or whoever is doing the action of the verb. The subject is often the first word in a sentence, but not always. Every sentence needs a subject (or more than one). To find the subject, first find the verb and ask who is doing the action.

Examples: 1. The **man** tied his shoes. (The subject is *man*.)

2. **Everyone** is going to the movies. (The subject is *everyone*.)

3. **Who** is knocking at the door? (The subject is *who*.)

4. After school, **she and I** always do our homework. (The subject is *she and I*; more than one subject is called a **compound** subject.)

5. Do **you** know who is at the door? (The subject is *you*.)

10. Predicates

The predicate of the sentence is the verb. The verb, along with its helping verbs, is called the **simple predicate.** The complete predicate is actually the rest of the sentence after the subject, but it is most important to know that the predicate is the verb. **Every sentence needs at least one verb.**

Examples: In the examples in Section 9, the predicates are 1. *tied,* 2. *is going,* 3. *is knocking,* 4. *do,* and 5. *know.*

11. Objects

There are two kinds of objects a sentence might have: direct and indirect. (Yes, there are also objects of prepositions; refer to Section 6). A sentence does not need an object at all. **A sentence needs only a subject and a verb to make it a complete sentence.** A sentence can have one kind of object, both kinds of objects, or no object at all. Objects are always nouns or pronouns, just like subjects. Direct objects receive the action of the verb. Ask **what?** or **who?** after the verb, and you will find the direct object. Indirect objects come between the verb and the direct object. You cannot have an indirect object without a direct object, but you can have a direct object without an indirect object. Examples will help here!

> ***Examples:*** 1. I threw the **ball** at James. (The direct object is ***ball***—threw what?)
>
> 2. Jane ate three **pieces** of cake. (The direct object is ***pieces,*** not ***cake***—ate what?)
>
> 3. I gave her a **gift**. (***Gift*** is the direct object—gave what? The indirect object is ***her.***)
>
> 4. Mom baked me a **cake.** (The direct object is ***cake***—baked what? The indirect object is ***me.***)

Predicate Words

Linking verbs (refer back to Section 3) do not have objects. They have **predicate adjectives** and **predicate nominatives** (nouns).

> ***Examples:*** 1. I am a writer. (***Am*** is a linking verb, so ***writer*** is not an object. Since ***writer*** is a noun, it is called a **predicate nominative.**)
>
> 2. I am happy. (***Am*** is a linking verb, so there is no object. Since ***happy*** is an adjective, it is called a **predicate adjective.**)

Note: Linking verbs connect the words before and after them. They function as an "equal" sign in the sentence. The subject and the predicate word are equal. In the above examples, *I* is the "same" as ***writer*** and ***happy.*** However, when there is an **action** verb, there is no linking of words before and after the verb. In the example **I threw the ball,** *threw* is not linking *I* and ***ball.*** I am not a ball!

---

12. Phrases

A phrase is a small group of words that go together. It is never a complete sentence, and it never has both a subject and a verb. It might have a noun and it might have a verb, but not both. Phrases add information and variety to your writing. In Section 3 we discussed **verb phrases** (the verb and its helping verbs). Here are some other common types of phrases:

1. Prepositional phrases tell where or when and contain a preposition and its object (a noun or a pronoun).

> I put it **on the table.**

> She is **at school.**

> **During the movie** the baby cried.

2. Infinitive phrases consist of the word **to** followed by a verb. (Note that **to** is not a preposition here because it is followed by a verb, not an object).

> I want **to go** home now.

> It is time **to take** the test.

3. Participial phrases contain a participle, which is a form of a verb used as an adjective. They usually end in **-ing** or are a past tense.

> **Running quickly,** I got to school late anyway.

> Dad, **driving the car,** wasn't listening.

> I looked at the **newly built** school.

4. Appositive phrases add information to a noun or pronoun and are usually enclosed in commas.

> Ann, **my neighbor,** is from Florida.

> The dress, **white with stripes,** is new.

> Ben, **my oldest brother,** is in college.

13. Clauses

A clause, like a phrase, is a group of words. However, a clause has both a subject and a verb. There are two main kinds of clauses, **dependent** and **independent.** An **independent** clause is a sentence, so we don't need to worry about those. A **dependent** clause, however, is not a complete sentence, so make sure you don't write one as a sentence. There are two types of dependent clauses, **adverb** and **adjective.** It is really not important that you know the difference, but adjective clauses describe nouns, and adverb clauses describe verbs.

1. Adjective clauses always start with the words **who, which, that, whom,** or **whose** (relative pronouns).

> John, **who is my neighbor,** is on vacation. (**Who** is the subject and **is** is the verb. The clause describes John.)

> The dress **that I bought** is in my closet. (**I** is the subject and **bought** is the verb. The clause describes the dress.)

2. Adverb clauses start with words such as **if, when, although, because, whenever,** and **since.** (They are called **subordinate** conjunctions.) These clauses can be either at the beginning or at the end of a sentence.

> **Because I was late,** I missed the bus.

> I missed the bus **because I was late.**

> **Although I can cook,** I cannot bake well.

- -
Note: When you take the dependent clause off the sentence, you still have a complete sentence left.
- -

Helpful Hint! Notice that there is no comma before **because** (and the other subordinating conjunctions) when the clause is at the end of the sentence. When you put the clause at the beginning of the sentence, you do use a comma.

14. Types of Sentences

There are four types of sentences, and there are also four structures for sentences. Here are the four types of sentences:

1. **Declarative sentences** are statements:

   I went to the basketball game yesterday.

2. **Interrogative sentences** are questions:

   Which teams played yesterday?

3. **Imperative sentences** are commands:

   Let me know next time you go to the game.

4. **Exclamatory sentences** express excitement:

   I just got tickets for the World Series!

- -
Note: Usually, there is no stated subject in a command. The command generally begins with a verb, for example, "**Clean** your room." The command actually means "**You** clean your room." The subject of any command is *you,* but it usually does not appear in the sentence.
- -

Sentence Structures

Sentences are made up of one or more clauses. Remember that a clause is a group of words that has a subject and a verb. Some clauses are complete sentences and can stand on their own. Other clauses cannot stand on their own; they are not complete thoughts, and they must be added to an independent clause, which is a complete sentence. Here are the four sentence structures:

Simple sentence

A simple sentence is **one independent clause.** Here are some simple sentences:

> Jack and Jill went up the hill.

In winter I tend to sleep more than in summer. (Although this sentence is fancier and has some prepositional phrases, it has only one verb and one clause.)

Compound sentence

A compound sentence is **two or more simple sentences** (or independent clauses) joined by one of those FANBOYS conjunctions (**for, and, nor, but, or, yet,** and **so**). Here are some compound sentences:

I ate my dinner, and I went to bed. Notice how each of the underlined sections is a sentence all by itself.

The dog ate the sofa, the cat tore the curtains, and the bird threw seeds everywhere. (There are three independent clauses in this compound sentence.)

Complex sentence

A complex sentence contains an independent clause and one or more dependent (adverb or adjective) clauses.

Because I was late, they left without me. (The dependent clause is underlined. The other clause is a complete sentence: **They left without me.**)

The woman, who was eating pizza, spilled her coffee. (The adjective clause is in the middle of the sentence. The independent clause is **the woman spilled her coffee,** a complete sentence on its own.)

Compound-complex sentences

These sentences contain two or more independent clauses (compound sentence) and at least one dependent clause: a combination of the complex and compound sentences.

I ate my pizza, which was getting cold, and I drank my juice. The two independent clauses are underlined. The dependent adjective clause is in the middle.

15. Not a Sentence: Fragments and Run-Ons

One of the most important things to know when you are writing is the difference between a sentence, a fragment, and a run-on. You must write in complete sentences and avoid run-on sentences and fragments. Run-ons and fragments are grammatically incorrect!

A sentence is a complete thought. It can be really short or really long. All it really needs is a subject and a verb. Here are some examples of sentences:

1. He ran.

2. He ran and ran and ran and ran and ran and ran and ran, and then he stopped.

3. Because I have no money, I cannot go to the movies.

A sentence fragment is not a sentence, but sometimes people think it is. A fragment is not a complete thought. Sometimes subordinate clauses are written as sentences, but they **are not.** Here are some samples of fragments or incomplete sentences. Do not use them in your writing!

1. Because I have no money. (This is **not** a complete thought. It is fine to add it to a sentence, as shown in the sentence examples above, but it cannot stand on its own.)

2. And I went with my friend. (Do not begin a sentence with **and, so, but,** or **or.**)

3. If I try really hard. (This is another subordinate clause that cannot stand on its own.)

A run-on sentence is another writing mistake. Here is a run-on:

We went to the movies, our friends went to the museum.

A run-on contains more than one complete sentence without proper punctuation. Two complete thoughts (sentences) must be separated in one of these three ways:

1. Put a period between them and start the second one with a capital letter.

We went to the movies. Our friends went to the museum.

2. Put a semicolon between them if the two sentences are closely related.

We went to the movies; our friends went to the museum.

3. Put a FANBOYS conjunction (***for, and, nor, but, or, yet, so***) between them.

We went to the movies, and our friends went to the museum. (Use a comma before the conjunction unless the whole sentence is very short.)

- -
Note: The word ***then*** is not a conjunction, and it cannot be used to join two sentences together unless you also use a conjunction.
- -

Do not ever separate two complete sentences with just a comma! That is a run-on (called a comma splice). It is wrong!

16. Sentence Variety Patterns

What is sentence variety? Structuring your sentences in different ways makes your writing more interesting. For example, instead of using all simple sentences (see Section 14) with the subject at the beginning of the sentence, you can use a variety of sentence patterns, including some complex and compound sentences. Here are some sentence patterns. You learned most of this information in Sections 12 and 13.

1. Start with a prepositional phrase: **On Wednesday** we went to the movies.

(Notice that you don't need a comma after a prepositional phrase that begins a sentence unless it is long or you use two prepositional phrases in a row, for example, **"On Wednesday after lunch,"**)

2. Start with an adverb clause: **After the movie was over,** we had dinner.

3. Start with an infinitive phrase: **To get into the movie,** we had to leave the house early.

4. Use an adjective clause: The movie, **which opened yesterday,** was crowded.

5. Use an appositive: The movie, **Star Wars,** was very popular when it came out.

6. Begin with a participial phrase: **Driving home,** we talked about how great the movie was!

7. Begin with a gerund: (**Gerund** is a new term. A gerund is a verb with an **-ing** ending that is used as a noun, for example, as the subject of a sentence): **Going** to movies is my favorite hobby.

Helpful Hint! How dull it would be to write the sentences above as simple sentences starting with subjects each time! Take a look . . .

We went to the movies on Wednesday. We had dinner after the movie. We had to leave the house early to get in. The movie was crowded. It opened yesterday. The movie was Star Wars. It was very popular when it first came out. We talked about how great the movie was when we were driving home. I really like going to the movies.

Chapter 3

The Basics:
Punctuation
and Capitalization

*The skill of writing is to create a context
in which other people can think.*

Edwin Schlossberg

Punctuation marks are those symbols in writing that let you know where sentences end and when to pause or ask a question. Without punctuation marks it would be nearly impossible to read a paragraph or a page of a book. Common punctuation marks include periods, commas, question marks, quotation marks, exclamation points, semicolons, colons, hyphens, and dashes.

Chapter 3 Quiz:
How Much Do You Know
About Punctuation and Capitalization?

Take this quiz before you read Chapter 3. The answers are on the back of this page.

1. Imperative sentences generally end with a(n)
   a. question mark   b. period   c. exclamation point   d. quote

2. I was born in Ohio and my brother was born in Utah.
   Place a comma in the correct place in the sentence, if necessary.

3. The girls and their mother went to the mall yesterday.
   Place a comma in the correct place in the sentence, if necessary.

4. 14 Baker Street Middletown New York 10051
   Place all the necessary commas in the address.

5. I ordered the steak __ my friend ordered pizza.
   Which mark belongs in the blank?
   a. comma   b. period   c. semicolon   d. hyphen

6. I brought shoes, a hat, a jacket, and socks.
   Place the colon in this sentence if it needs one.

7. My cousin—she just got back from studying in Paris is coming to visit next week.
   Put the other dash where it belongs in the sentence.

8. She asked, Are you going to the prom with Tony?
   Put the quotation marks in the correct places.

9. Titles of books are written in
   a. italics   b. quotes   c. boldface   d. all caps

10. the golden gate bridge is one of many tourist attractions i will see when we visit california this summer.
    How many words in this sentence need to be capitalized?
    a. 4   b. 5   c. 6   d. 7

Answers to Chapter 3 Quiz

1. Imperative sentences generally end with a
   a. question mark   ***b. period***   c. exclamation point   d. quote

2. I was born in Ohio, and my brother was born in Utah.
   Place a comma in the correct place in the sentence, if necessary.

3. The girls and their mother went to the mall yesterday.
   Place a comma in the correct place in the sentence, if necessary.
   There is no comma in this sentence.

4. 14 Baker Street, Middletown, New York 10051
   Place all the necessary commas in the address.

5. I ordered the steak __ my friend ordered pizza.
   Which mark belongs in the blank?
   a. comma   b. period   ***c. semicolon***   d. hyphen

6. I brought shoes, a hat, a jacket, and socks.
   Place the colon in this sentence if it needs one.
   There is no colon in this sentence.

7. My cousin—she just got back from studying in Paris—is coming to visit next week.
   Put the other dash where it belongs in the sentence.

8. She asked, "Are you going to the prom with Tony?"
   Put the quotation marks in the correct place.

9. Titles of books are written in
   a. italics   b. quotes   c. boldface   d. all caps

10. **T**he **G**olden **G**ate **B**ridge is one of many tourist attractions **I** will see when we visit **C**alifornia this summer.

How many words in this sentence need to be capitalized?
   a. 4   b. 5   ***c. 6***   d. 7

10 correct: Grammar Whiz!!
8–9 correct: Very Good!
6–7 correct: Pretty Good!
5 or fewer correct: Need Some Practice!

17. Periods and Other Ending Punctuation

By ending punctuation, we mean the marks that come at the end of a sentence. Every sentence needs some punctuation at the end. Most sentences have a period at the end.

Statements, or declarative sentences, have a period at the end. Most sentences are declarative.

Example: He went to the party with me.

Imperative sentences, or commands, also have a period at the end.

Example: Take the book to school.

Interrogative sentences, or questions, have a question mark at the end.

Example: Did you go to the party last night?

Exclamatory sentences (sentences that express excitement) have an exclamation point at the end.

Example: There's a fire in the kitchen!

Interjections are also often followed by an exclamation point.

Example: Wow! Did you see that car?

If you have a quote, the period always goes **inside** the quotation marks.

Example: He said, "I always shop on Wednesdays."

Helpful Hint! Question marks and exclamation points go inside the quotes if they are part of the quote, and outside if they are not part of the quote.

Examples: "Do you have a pencil?" she asked. (The quoted sentence is a question.)

Did you say "I have no pencil"? (The whole sentence is a question, not the quoted part.)

---

18. Commas

Commas have about 700 rules! Well, maybe not 700, but commas have many rules. We will discuss the most common uses of commas here.

1. Series: Commas are used after each item in a series, including right before the word **and** or **or** (before the last item in the series).

> **Examples:**   I brought shoes, socks, a jacket, and a sweater.
>
> She went to the park, to the mall, and to the grocery store.

2. Compound sentences: A compound sentence is two (or more) complete sentences connected by a conjunction such as **and** or **or.** Short compound sentences don't need the comma.

> **Examples:**   She brought her brother home, and she made him dinner.
>
> I am hungry and I am thirsty. (Sentence is too short to need the comma.)

- -

Note: Both sides of the conjunction need to be complete sentences; otherwise, the sentence is *not* compound, and you don't need a comma.

> **Example:**   She brought her brother home and made him dinner. (**Made him dinner** is not a complete sentence; it has no subject. Do not use a comma.)

- -

3. After introductory clauses: If a sentence starts with one of those dependent clauses we talked about in Section 13, use a comma.

> **Example:**   **Because he is a good dog,** I gave him a treat.
> (Note that if you turn the sentence around and write
> *I gave him a treat because he is a good dog,*
> there is no comma. Go figure!)

4. After long introductory phrases: If a sentence begins with a long phrase, for example, a participial phrase, use a comma.

> **Example:**   **Stretching out comfortably on the sofa,** my cat fell asleep.

5. After multiple introductory prepositional phrases. If more than one prepositional phrase starts a sentence, use a comma.

Examples: **After midnight** we went to the movies.

After midnight in the city, we went to the movies.

6. Before and after words, phrases, and clauses that interrupt a sentence: Note that when you remove whatever is between commas, the sentence should still make sense.

Examples: I am**, therefore,** going with you.

The story is**, in my opinion,** false.

This shirt**, which was on sale,** is ripped.

7. In dates and addresses: In addresses, there is a comma after the street and between the city and the state (if you are writing the address on an envelope, there is no comma after the street). **There is no comma between the state and the zip code!**

Example: She lives at 30 Mill Street, Philadelphia, PA 30409.

In dates there is a comma after the day of the week and after the number of the day in the month. If there is no date specified, there is no comma between the month and year.

Examples: She was born on Tuesday, March 23, 2006.

I graduated in May 2007.

Helpful Hint! There is **_never_** a comma between the subject and the verb of a sentence. Don't do it!

Example: The girls, went to the mall yesterday. **Wrong!**

The girls went to the mall yesterday. **Right!**

Another Helpful Hint! Use a comma whenever not using one would cause the reader confusion.

Example: Toy dogs and terriers, and hunting dogs and sporting dogs were two of the groupings at the show.

19. Semicolons

Semicolons are not too complicated. Unlike commas, semicolons really have only three usage rules. Semicolons, by the way, look like this: **;**

Here are the rules:

1. Use a semicolon in a **compound sentence** (two sentences joined together with the conjunctions ***and, or, nor, yet, so, but, for***) when you don't want to use the conjunction. To use a semicolon, two sentences must be somewhat closely related.

> **Example:** I ordered the steak; my friend ordered the salmon.
>
> You can also write this sentence: I ordered the steak, and my friend ordered the salmon. (You can also use a period: I ordered the steak. My friend ordered the salmon.) Do not use both the conjunction and the semicolon in this situation. Use **either** the conjunction or the semicolon.

Note: Do not begin the second part of the sentence (after the semicolon) with a capital letter!

2. Use a semicolon in a compound sentence where a conjunction **is** used, but where there is a series in one of the parts of the sentence.

> **Example:** I saw Jenny, Joe, Mark, and Sam; and I didn't see Jim. (This use of the semicolon simply makes things clearer and easier to read—and **clarity** is the purpose of punctuation.)

3. Try to figure out this sentence:

Mr. Abbott, my Spanish teacher, my math teacher, Mrs. White, a parent, and Mr. Bloom are chaperoning the dance.

Can you tell how many people we are talking about here? How about now?

Mr. Abbott, my Spanish teacher; my math teacher; Mrs. White, a parent; and Mr. Bloom are chaperoning the dance.

Four people are chaperoning. The third rule of the semicolon is to use it in a series if one or more of the items in the series have commas. Follow **each** item but the last with a semicolon even if some of the items don't have commas in them. For example, **my math teacher** is standing by itself, but still has semicolons around it for consistency. Each separate item has a semicolon after it.

20. Colons

There are not many rules for colons. The most common use of a colon is to introduce a list.

1. Use a colon to introduce a list in a sentence. Many times the words **follow** or **following** are used in the introduction before the colon, but not necessarily. Here are some examples:

a. Please bring the following items: a coat, shoes, a hat, and an umbrella.

b. These are some of the items to bring: a coat, shoes, a hat, and an umbrella.

Helpful Hint! Do not use a colon if the sentence reads fine as a sentence. In the examples above, if you took the colon out, the words would not read correctly as a sentence. However, look at this sentence:

Please bring a coat, shoes, a hat, and an umbrella.

You would **never** put a colon after **bring** because that would cut the sentence up. Do not put a colon between a verb and list items!

---

2. Colons are also used to introduce a vertical list. Here is an example:

Please bring the following items:

- a coat
- shoes
- a hat
- an umbrella

Once again, even in a vertical list, you don't put a colon after a verb when the list items complete the sentence.

Please bring

- a coat
- shoes
- a hat
- an umbrella

3. Colons can also be used to separate two sentences if the second sentence follows from the first (as opposed to using a semicolon when the sentences are simply closely related). This is not a very common usage and can usually be avoided by simply using two sentences or rewriting.

> **Example:**   There is a meeting on Friday: layoffs and new projects will be discussed at that time.

If you used a semicolon instead, that would be fine too. Whether you use a semicolon or a colon, do not capitalize the second part of the sentence.

4. The other uses for a colon are, of course, in time (9:50 a.m.) and after the salutation (greeting) of a business letter (Dear Sirs:).

21. Parentheses, Brackets, and Braces

Parentheses ( ) are used to enclose information that isn't of major importance. You can use parentheses around a single word, a phrase, or a complete sentence. You can put the parentheses within the sentence, or, if the material in parentheses is a complete sentence, you can even put it on its own. Here are some examples. Notice the punctuation because it can be confusing if your material in parentheses is a sentence.

> **Examples:**   1. Joe Moon (1915–1970) was a great artist in my town.
>
> 2. Joe Moon (he was my uncle) was a wonderful artist.
>
> 3. Joe Moon was a wonderful artist (he was also my uncle).
>
> 4. Joe Moon was a wonderful artist. (He was my uncle and taught me how to paint.)

In Example 2, the enclosed material is a complete sentence, but it doesn't require either a capital at the beginning or a period at the end because it is included in the sentence. Example 3 is the same, but the parenthetical information is at the end. Notice that the period goes outside of the parentheses. In Example 4 the parenthetical information is its own sentence and is placed outside the other sentence. The original sentence has its own period. Therefore, the sentence in parentheses would have a capital letter to begin it and a period to end it.

Brackets [ ] are not used that much. They can be used to add an explanation to quoted material. In this case, always use brackets instead of parentheses.

> ***Example:***   "I love this [dress], and it was designed especially for this occasion."

In the example, the word ***dress*** was not in the quote, but it is needed for the reader to understand the quote.

Brackets are also used to further explain information that is already in parentheses. If you need parentheses inside of parentheses, you use brackets **inside the parentheses.**

> ***Example:***   Turn to page 65 (the bottom of the page [Review B]), and read the instructions.

Braces { } Don't even worry about it!

22. Hyphens (-) and Dashes (– and —)

Hyphen - (shortest)

En dash – (medium)

Em dash — (longest)

Okay, so what's the difference among these three?

Hyphen

A hyphen is used in some compound words (two words that are put together as one word); it is also used when you split a word at the end of a line.

1. Some compound words are hyphenated. There is no real general rule as to when you hyphenate a word. Generally, when a word is new, it is two separate words; as the word becomes more common, it becomes hyphenated. When it becomes really common, it is often written as one word.

Example: Web site, Web-site, and Website. The best thing to do is look in the dictionary if you can; otherwise, take your best guess.

Helpful Hint! There are two common beginnings to compound words: **self** and **well**. For example, **well known, well liked, well done, self motivated, self assured.**

Here is what you do with these words:

This is a **self-study** course. The course is **self study.**

He is a **well-known** painter. The painter is very **well known.**

If the compound word with **self-** or **well-** comes before the noun that it describes, it is hyphenated. If it comes after the verb, it is **not** hyphenated.

Another common hyphenation: He is a **ten-year-old boy**. The boy is a **ten year old.** (Use hyphens if the description comes **before** the noun (**boy**).

Here is another example: *Man* is a one-syllable word. The word *man* has one syllable.

---

2. A hyphen is used to split a word when you don't have room to write the whole word on the line. With computers, this problem is pretty much outdated. However, if you are writing or typing, and you do have to split a word at the end of a line, you must split it between syllables. This means you cannot **ever** split a one-syllable word. You can look up where the syllables split in the dictionary. If you have no dictionary, split the word so that you can pronounce the sections that are on each line. There is usually a vowel in each syllable. If the word has a double consonant, such as **happen,** the word is split between the double consonant (**hap pen**).

En Dash

You can probably use the same dash for all your dash needs, but there is a difference. The **en dash** is the shorter of the two dashes. Some people just hit the hyphen twice. Sometimes the computer puts them together for you. You can also press the Control key and the hyphen on the number pad in Word for Windows, or press the Command key and the hyphen on the number pad in Word for the Macintosh to get an en dash. The main use of an en dash is to indicate a range of numbers or dates, for example, pages **64–67.** The en dash is also used to make a subtraction sign.

Em Dash

The em dash is the long one that you use to indicate a break in your sentence. You can use Insert Symbol in Word to find an em dash. You can sometimes use parentheses instead of a dash (and sometimes maybe even commas), but generally an em dash is used to indicate a bigger break in your thoughts. The sentence should still make sense if you take the text between the dashes out.

Example: Our vacation—if we can afford to take one this year—will be a trip to Europe.

Helpful Hint! There are no spaces before and after hyphens or dashes.

---

23. Italics

Italics are those slanted words you sometimes see in books or magazines. You cannot write by hand in italics; you can use italics for printed material only. To italicize something when you are writing by hand, you underline it instead.

1. Italicize titles of big things. By **big things,** I mean book titles, titles of plays, titles of operas, titles of television series, titles of CDs, and other complete works. Parts of these works, or **shorter things,** are quoted. For example, chapter titles, short story titles, titles of television series' episodes, and titles of songs are in quotes.

2. Use italics when you are referring to a letter, a number, or a word as itself.

Examples:　My name begins with the letter *A*.

The word *terrarium* has always been difficult for me to spell.

My lucky numbers are 2 and *8*.

24. Quotation Marks (" ") and Single Quotation Marks (' ')

Quotation marks have two main uses: to enclose direct quotations (the exact words someone says) and to enclose titles of short works.

1. **Enclosing titles:** In Section 23 we discussed putting titles of books, plays, television series, CDs, operas, and other long works in *italics* (or underlining them in handwritten text).

For short works, such as short stories, chapter titles, a single episode of a TV series, or a song, use quotation marks.

2. **Direct quotes:** You must use quotation marks around direct quotes, or the exact words that someone says.

Examples:　John said, "I am hungry." (direct quote)

John said that he was hungry. (not a direct quote, so no quotation marks)

Here are some rules to follow when quoting:

1. The direct quote starts with a capital letter.

Example:　He said, **"W**e want our pie."

2. In a split quotation, the second part does **not** begin with a capital letter.

Example: .　"I want my pie," he said, "**a**nd the rest of my lunch!"

3. Notice that periods are not used to set off quoted sentences from the rest of the sentence.

Example:　**"I want my pie,"** he said. (comma after *pie* is correct) It is not "I want my pie." he said.

4. Periods and commas are always placed inside quotes. Question marks and exclamation points can go either inside or outside quotes. If they are part of the quote, they are placed inside the quote. If they are part of the entire sentence, they are placed outside the quotes. Here are some examples of punctuation with quotes:

Examples: "I want my pie," he said.

He said, "I want my pie."

Did he say, "I want my pie"? (Notice there is no period after *pie*. Only one piece of punctuation is used, the question mark. The question mark applies to the whole sentence.)

He asked, "Where is my pie?" (Here, the question mark is part of the quote, so it is placed inside the quotation marks.)

"I lost my pie!" he exclaimed.

It scared me when he said, "I want my pie"! (The whole sentence is an exclamation, not the quote.)

Did he ask, "Where is my pie?" (Here, **both** the quote and the whole sentence are questions. Use one question mark, and put it before the quotation marks.)

Single Quotes

Use single quotes when you need to put quotes inside of quotes.

Examples: She said, "I read the short story 'Mother and Me' for my essay." (The short story title needs quotes around it.)

She said, "I read the short story 'Mother and Me.'" (There is a single quote for the poem and double quotes for the quote, so there are three quotes at the end of the sentence.)

25. Capitalization

Yikes! There are so many rules for capitalization! Basically, capitalize the names of specific people, places, and things (proper nouns).

Examples: Don't capitalize **boy,** but capitalize **Robert.**

Don't capitalize **school,** but capitalize **Blair High School.**

Don't capitalize **summer,** but capitalize **Fourth of July.**

Places and things that contain more than one word, such as Fourth of July, follow the same capitalization rules as titles (see Section 95).

In a nutshell, here are the rules for capitalization:

1. Capitalize the first word of every sentence.

2. Capitalize the first word of the greeting or closing of a letter (for example, Dear Sirs, Yours truly [**Sirs** is a title, so it is capitalized too]).

3. Capitalize the pronoun **I.**

4. Capitalize proper nouns, including people's and animal's names (for example, Julie, Fido, Spot, Mr. Jones).

5. Capitalize cities, states, countries, continents, oceans, islands, streets, mountains, forests, and regions of the country (for example, San Francisco, Texas, United States, North America, Atlantic Ocean, Mississippi River, Main Street, the Alps, Yosemite National Park, New England, and the Middle East).

Helpful Hint! Do not capitalize north, south, east, and west when they indicate direction. **Do** capitalize them if they are used to name a region.

Example: She is from the South.

I need to travel south on this highway.

---

6. Capitalize the names of clubs, teams, and government bodies (for example, Parent-Teacher Organization, Boston Celtics, Middletown City Council).

7. Capitalize holidays, events, and historical periods (for example, Fourth of July, Labor Day, Oklahoma State Fair, Revolutionary War).

8. Capitalize the names of nationalities, races, and peoples (for example, French, African American, Navajo).

9. Capitalize businesses and brand names (for example, Central Bank, Tasty Soup, Sally's Cleaning).

10. Capitalize the names of ships, trains, spacecraft, and aircraft (for example, the Mayflower, Pioneer 10).

11. Capitalize the names of buildings and other structures (for example, Bristle Building, Golden Gate Bridge, Towne Theater).

12. Capitalize the names of awards, monuments, and memorials (for example, Academy Award, Lincoln Memorial, Newbury Medal).

13. Capitalize religions, holy books, and some deities (for example, Christianity, Judaism, Hinduism, Protestant, the Bible, God). Note that the word *god* is not capitalized when it refers to a mythological god.

14. Capitalize planets, stars, constellations, and other heavenly bodies (for example, Mars, Orion's Belt, the Milky Way). Note that sun, moon, and earth are usually not capitalized.

15. Capitalize a person's title if it comes before the name (for example, Mr. Jones, Dr. West, Mayor Dunster).

16. Capitalize a word that shows a family relationship if it comes before the name or is used in place of the name (for example, **Aunt Mary,** but **my aunt; Mom,** but **my mom**).

17. Capitalize most words in titles (see Section 95).

Chapter 4

Things Not to Use

Speak properly, and in as few words as you can, but always plainly;
for the end of speech is not ostentation, but to be understood.

William Penn
English religious leader and colonist (1644–1718)

This chapter contains some of the things you just shouldn't do when you write, particularly when you write in school or business. Academic and business writing is formal, and you don't want to write the way you might text or talk to your friends.

Chapter 4 Quiz:
How Much Do You Know
About These Things Not to Use?

Take this quiz before you read Chapter 4. The answers are on the back of this page.

Which of the following sentences are both correct (grammar and punctuation) and appropriate for a business letter or a school essay? Circle Yes or No.

1. I am buying a really cool house.   Yes   No

2. I am not going anywheres for vacation.   Yes   No

3. I would of gone if I had money.   Yes   No

4. Firstly, I am qualified for this position.   Yes   No

5. There are more boy's in this class than girl's.   Yes   No

6. And there is a meeting on Thursday.   Yes   No

7. Try and come on the field trip if you can.   Yes   No

8. I haven't got a job.   Yes   No

9. Elaine, has just been promoted to manager.   Yes   No

10. You should've told me you couldn't come.   Yes   No

Answers to Chapter 4 Quiz

None of the sentences are correct and appropriate!

1. I am buying a really cool house.   Yes   **No**
   Cool is slang.

2. I am not going anywheres for vacation.   Yes   **No**
   Anywhere never has an **s** at the end.

3. I would of gone if I had money.   Yes   **No**
   Would of should be **would have.**

4. Firstly, I am qualified for this position.   Yes   **No**
   Firstly should be **first.**

5. There are more boy's in this class than girl's.   Yes   **No**
   Plural nouns do not have apostrophes in them.

6. And there is a meeting on Thursday.   Yes   **No**
   Do not start a sentence with a conjunction (**and**).

7. Try and come on the field trip if you can.   Yes   **No**
   Try and should be **try to.**

8. I haven't got a job.   Yes   **No**
   I don't have a job is correct. Don't use **got** here.

9. Elaine, has just been promoted to manager.   Yes   **No**
   Do not put a comma between the subject and the verb.

10. You should've told me you couldn't come.   Yes   **No**
    Avoid using contractions in formal writing.

10 correct: Grammar Whiz!!
8–9 correct: Very Good!
6–7 correct: Pretty Good!
5 or fewer correct: Need Some Practice!

26. Dead Words

Eliminate dead words from your writing and, if necessary, use a thesaurus to find a better word! Here are some **dead** words to avoid:

- **A lot**—too informal. However, if you must occasionally use it, it is two separate words (not **alot**)!

- **Good** and **bad**—too common. Come on—you can do better! Same goes for **great**!

- **Stuff, things, bunch**—Be specific! Use **bunch** only when you are talking about bananas!

- **Nice, fun** and other boring adjectives (by the way, **funner** and **funnest** are not words!)

- **Really, very,** and other boring adverbs. Instead of these two words, use **unusually, fully, extensively, certainly, extremely, incredibly, exceptionally, remarkably, particularly,** or **exceedingly.**

- **Cool, awesome,** and all slang and overused words

- **Gonna, shoulda, woulda, coulda**—these are not words at all!

- **Nite, lite,** and other incorrect shorthand spellings

- **Have got**—just **have** is enough! Example: **I have a dog.** not **I have got a dog.**

27. Anywheres, Anyways

Anywheres, nowheres, somewheres, and **anyways** are not words. There is never an **s** at the end of these words! (The same is also true for **ways** if you are talking about distance: **I have a long way to go,** Not **I have a long ways to go.**)

28. As yet

Do not use **as yet. Yet** is enough.

Use: **I don't know <u>yet</u>.**

Don't use: **I don't know <u>as yet</u>.**

29. Wasted Words

The fact that is a wasted phrase. You don't need those words at all.

Use:	**You should know that I am moving away.**
Don't use:	**You should know the fact that I am moving away.**
Use:	**I am the chairperson.**
Don't use:	**The fact that I am the chairperson is important.**

Hopefully, everyone knows by now that you don't put the pronoun after the noun.

| Wrong: | **John <u>he</u> went to the store**. |
| Right: | **John went to the store.**   OR
He went to the store. |

30. *Kind of, Sort of*

Don't use ***kind of*** and ***sort of.*** And don't <u>**ever**</u> use ***kinda*** and ***sorta***!

| Don't use: | **The flowers are kind of wilted.** |
| Use: | **The flowers are wilted** or **The flowers are slightly wilted.** |

31. A Comma to Separate Sentences

You have already read about this in Section 15. **Never** separate two sentences with a comma! You need a period or a semicolon to separate two sentences. Otherwise, you have a **run-on,** otherwise known as a **comma splice.**

Don't use:	**I went to the movies, my brother could not go with me.**
Use:	**I went to the movies. My brother could not go with me.** OR
	I went to the movies; my brother could not go with me. OR

I went to the movies, but my brother could not go with me.

32. Contractions

Avoid contractions in formal writing. Spell the words out. *I'm* should be *I am. You're* should be *you are.* Never use a contraction of *is.* For example, write out *he is;* don't use *he's* in formal writing.

33. *Could of/Should of/Would of*

Do not use *could of, should of,* and *would of.* Of course, it goes without saying (and we already said it) that we don't use *coulda, shoulda,* or *woulda* (or *gonna*)!

The correct way to write these phrases is as follows:

Could have

Should have

Would have

Always use *have,* not *of,* with these words.

34. Conjunction to Start a Sentence

Do not start a sentence with a FANBOYS conjunction. These conjunctions include *for, and, nor, but, or, yet,* and *so.* Do not begin a sentence with any of those words!

You can, however, begin a word with a subordinating conjunction such as *because, although, if, whenever,* and *since.* Just make sure that the adverb clause they introduce is followed or preceded by a complete sentence:

Correct: **Because I have no money, I cannot go to the movies with you.**

Incorrect: **Because I have no money.** (not a complete sentence)

Correct:	**If I clean my room, I can go out to play.**
Incorrect:	**If I clean my room.** (not a complete sentence)

35. *Each and Every*

Each and every is redundant. **Every** or **each** is enough:

Correct:	**Study your notes <u>every</u> time there is a test.**
Incorrect:	**Study your notes <u>each and every</u> time there is a test.**

36. Abbreviations

Do not use abbreviations such as **e.g., i.e.,** or **etc.,** in formal writing. Use the spelled out versions. Here they are:

etc. (et cetera) means "and so on" or "and all the rest." Try to put all the items in the list and avoid using **etc.**

Correct:	**I brought shoes, a hat, a coat, a scarf, and long underwear.**
Incorrect:	**I brought shoes, a hat, a coat, etc.**

i.e. means "that is," so simply say "that is."

Correct:	**I returned that book, that is, the Spanish book, to the library yesterday.**
Incorrect:	**I returned that book, i.e., the Spanish book, to the library yesterday.**

e.g. means "for example," so just say "for example."

Correct:	**Take some winter clothes, for example, a hat, to the mountains.**
Incorrect:	**Take some winter clothes, e.g., a hat, to the mountains.**

In lists, memos, and informal writing you can use these abbreviations, but remember they are always preceded and followed by a comma.

37. *Firstly, Secondly, Thirdly, Lastly*

Do not use these words. Use *first, second, third, last, finally.*

38. Double Negatives

Most of us know not to use the old double negatives, but there are some double negatives that are not as obvious.

Some double negatives:

I don't have no money . . . should be **I don't have any money.**

I haven't got no money . . . should be **I don't have any money.**

I haven't barely any money . . . should be **I have barely any money.** (**Barely** is a negative.)

I haven't hardly begun . . . should be **I have hardly begun.** (**Hardly** is a negative.)

I could care less . . . Not correct! This should be **I couldn't care less.** (Think about the meaning. If you could care less, then you care some—which is probably not what you mean.)

39. *Try and*

Try and is incorrect. Use *try to.*

Correct: <u>**Try to**</u> **eat the vegetables.**

Incorrect: <u>**Try and**</u> **eat the vegetables.**

40. *Irregardless*

Irregardless is not a word. The correct word is regardless.

Example: **Regardless** of the consequences, I am going to sail around the world in my small boat.

41. Apostrophes in Plurals

There is **no apostrophe** in a plural noun!!

Incorrect: **There are many <u>dog's</u> in the room.**

Correct: **There are many <u>dogs</u> in the room.**

The only time you use an apostrophe in a plural is for numbers, letters, symbols, and words used as words.

Examples: A's, 6's, &'s, 1900's

How many *and*'s did you put in that sentence? (Note that the word used as a word is in italics. However, the apostrophe and the *s* are not.)

42. Comma Between Subject and Verb

I see this too often! Some people insist on putting a comma between the subject of the sentence and the verb (I know *you* don't!!). This is wrong and certainly not in the comma rules! The only time you would put a comma after the subject is if it is directly followed by an appositive phrase or clause between it and the verb.

Examples:

Incorrect: **The children, can play in this room.**

Correct: **The children can play in this room.**

Correct: **The children, who just arrived from daycare, can play in this room.** (The clause between the subject and the verb is set off with commas.)

Correct: **The children, my neighbors, can play in this room.** (The appositive phrase between the subject and the verb is set off with commas.)

43. Unclear Pronouns and Antecedents

First of all, what is an **antecedent**? In Section 2, we talked about pronouns. Pronouns substitute for a noun or other pronoun in a sentence. The **antecedent** is the noun (or pronoun) that the pronoun is replacing.

Examples: **Sue** took **her** book back to the library. The noun ***Sue*** is the antecedent for the pronoun ***her.*** (You wouldn't want to say, "Sue brought Sue's book back to the library.")

She took **her** book back to the library. The pronoun ***she*** is the antecedent of the pronoun ***her.***

When you use a pronoun, and the reader cannot tell what that pronoun refers to, you have an unclear antecedent. Common pronouns with unclear antecedents tend to be the pronouns ***this*** and ***which.***

Example: I had two papers to write during the weekend, and I also had a math test to study for. **This** made things difficult.

It isn't really clear what ***this*** refers to. The pronouns ***this*** and ***which*** should always refer to one noun or pronoun. They should not be used to represent a whole idea.

Incorrect: I had a really busy weekend. **This** made it difficult to study.

What made it difficult to study?

Correct: I couldn't study much because I had a busy weekend.   OR

My busy weekend made it difficult to study. (There are also other ways to write this idea.)

Incorrect: He is a really good friend, **which** is nice for me.

What is nice for you?

Correct: It is nice that he is a really good friend to me.

Also be careful with the pronoun *it.*

Incorrect:	This past weekend I went camping, swimming, and hiking. **It** was really nice.

What was really nice?

Correct:	This past weekend I went camping, swimming, and hiking. These activities were really fun.

44. *Got* Instead of *Have*

Do not use **got** when you mean **have.**

Examples:	**I don't got any books** . . . should be . . . **I don't have any books.**
	Have you got any money? . . . should be . . . **Do you have any money?**
	I got a new car for my birthday . . . is correct. (**Got** means **received** here.)

45. Redundancy: Repeating Yourself

Be careful when you write, and also when you speak, not to use words and phrases that are redundant, or to say the same thing twice. It is easier to catch these redundancies in writing than in speaking because in speaking you cannot go back and change things!

Here are some examples of redundancies:

1. **We cut the cost by 30 percent less.** If we cut the cost, of course it was less! You don't need the word *less* here. **We cut the cost by 30 percent** is just fine.

2. **It permeates through the air.** *Permeate* means "to pass through," so the word *through* is redundant. **It permeates the air** is enough.

3. **It is completely unique.** Something is either unique or it isn't. You don't need the word *completely.* **It is unique.**

4. **It is my personal opinion.** If it is your opinion, it is personal, so you don't need the word *personal* there. **It is my opinion.**

5. **I don't know whether or not she is coming with us.** You don't need to say *or not.* **I don't know whether she is coming with us.**

These are many more redundant words and phrases, so choose your words carefully. Just something to think about.

Chapter 5
Confusing Things

If the English language made any sense,
a catastrophe would be an apostrophe with fur.

Doug Larson
American Cartoonist

This chapter discusses words that are often confused.

Chapter 5 Quiz:
How Much Do You Know
About These Confusing Things?

Take this quiz before you read Chapter 5. The answers are on the back of this page.

Circle the correct choice for each sentence.

1. The competition (effected, affected) her.

2. I am feeling (alright, all right).

3. Divide the pizza (between, among) the three of us.

4. I feel (bad, badly) about my score on the test.

5. These colors (complement, compliment) each other.

6. He gave her and (me, I) a gift.

7. (Whom, Who) are you taking with you?

8. The cat is shedding (it's, its) fur.

9. I (lay, laid) down on the lounge chair yesterday.

10. I have (fewer, less) chores than my sister does.

11. Finish your dinner, and (then, than) we can go.

12. (Their, They're) coming with us.

13. (Who's, Whose) chair is this?

14. I bought some pretty (stationery, stationary).

15. I (set, sat) my backpack on the table.

Answers to Chapter 5 Quiz

1. The competition (effected, **affected**) her.

2. I am feeling (alright, **all right**).

3. Divide the pizza (between, **among**) the three of us.

4. I feel (**bad,** badly) about my score on the test.

5. These colors (**complement,** compliment) each other.

6. He gave her and (**me,** I) a gift.

7. (**Whom,** Who) are you taking with you?

8. The cat is shedding (it's, **its**) fur.

9. I (**lay,** laid) down on the lounge chair yesterday.

10. I have (**fewer,** less) chores than my sister does.

11. Finish your dinner, and (**then,** than) we can go.

12. (Their, **They're**) coming with us.

13. (Who's, **Whose**) chair is this?

14. I bought some pretty (**stationery,** stationary).

15. I (**set,** sat) my backpack on the table.

15 correct: Grammar Whiz!!
13–14 correct: Very Good!
11–12 correct: Pretty Good!
10 or fewer correct: Need Some Practice!

46. *Advice/Advise*

Advice (the *c* sounds like an *s*) is a noun. *Advise* (the *s* sounds like a *z*) is a verb. Here is the correct usage:

Examples: I gave my friend **advice** about his problem.

I **advised** my friend to talk to someone about his problem.

47. *Affect/Effect*

These two are tough! Each can be either a noun or a verb. The most common use is to use *affect* as a verb and *effect* as a noun. Here is the correct usage:

Examples: How does the hot weather **affect** you?

What **effect** does the hot weather have on you?

However, sometimes it is the other way around! *Effect* will be used as a verb, and *affect* will be used as a noun. *Affect* as a noun means *an attitude* or *way of acting.* Here is the correct usage:

Examples: He had a rather quiet **affect.** (Note that the word is pronounced differently as a noun. The first syllable is stressed, and the *a* is short like in the word *absent* (a′fekt).

The new President will try to **effect** some changes in the country.

48. *Already/All ready*

Already is an adverb. It refers to time. Here is the correct usage:

Examples: Did you get home **already**?

Are you **all ready** to go to the party?

49. *Alright/All right*

This one is easy! **Alright** is not a word, so you don't have to worry about it at all! Here is the correct usage:

Example: I asked the man if he was **all right** after the accident.

50. *Among/Between*

These two words are prepositions. Use **between** when you are talking about **two** things. Use **among** when there are **more than two.** Here is the correct usage:

Examples: Divide the pie **between** the two of you.

Divide the pie **among** the three of us.

So where is the verb?

51. *Bad/Badly*

Bad is an adjective, and **badly** is an adverb. Use **badly** if you are modifying an action verb. Use **bad** to modify a noun or after a linking verb (as a **predicate adjective;** refer to Section 11). Here is the correct usage:

Examples: I feel **bad** about the accident. (**Feel** is a linking verb, linking **I** and **bad. Bad** is describing the pronoun **I.**)

She performed **badly** on the test. (**Badly** is an adverb describing the action verb **performed.** *Performed how?* **Badly.**)

52. *Good/Well*

Good is an adjective, and **well** is an adverb. Therefore, use **well** if you are modifying an action verb. Use **good** to modify a noun or after a linking verb (as a predicate adjective). Here is the correct usage:

Examples: I feel **good** about my performance. (**Feel** is a linking verb. **Good** describes **I.**)

She did **well** on the test because she studied. (**Well** is an adverb describing the action word **did.** She did *how?* **Well!**)

53. *Compliment/Complement*

Compliment: Your dress is really pretty.

You look great today!

Those are **compliments** with an *i.*

Complement: This fruit sauce **complements** the meat.

Her dress **complements** her blue eyes.

Complement with an **e** means to go well with, or to show off well.

54. *Data*

Data is actually a plural word. The singular form is ***datum,*** but ***datum*** is rarely used. ***Data*** means information, and the plural use is generally fine (even with a singular verb).

Example: This **data** is quite interesting. (You wouldn't say ***the data are interesting*** even though ***are*** is the plural verb.)

55. *Desert/Dessert*

Dessert with the double **s** is the stuff you eat! And you can remember it because it is so good, you always want two!

Desert with the single **s** means that hot, dry place; it can also mean to leave.

Example: He **deserted** the **desert** after eating **dessert**!

56. *Further/Farther, Toward/Towards*

These words can be pretty confusing! ***Farther*** means *a greater distance.* ***Further*** means *additional.* Here is the correct usage:

Examples: My house is **farther** away from school than yours is.

I cannot run any **farther** than ten miles.

We can discuss this **further** later.

My essay needs **further** work.

Toward and ***towards*** mean the same thing. You can use either word, but ***toward*** is preferred.

57. *However* and *Therefore*

These two words are often punctuated incorrectly because each of them can be used in two different ways. Each word can be used as an interrupter in the middle of a sentence. Each word can also be used at the beginning of a sentence that is closely related to the previous sentence (often these two sentences are a compound sentence separated with a semicolon).

Examples:

1. The book, **however,** is not in the library. (You could leave out ***however,*** and the sentence would still make perfect sense.)

2. I couldn't find the book; **however,** I think the library has it. (Here, there are two separate sentences: ***I couldn't find the book*** is a sentence; ***I think the library has it*** is also a sentence. Therefore, you need a semicolon between them. You **cannot** use a comma instead of the semicolon; that would be a run-on sentence. (You could also use a period instead of the semicolon and make them two separate sentences. You would then use a capital ***H*** in ***however.***) ***However*** is generally followed by a comma.

3. I won't have the book, **therefore,** to help me. (You could easily leave out **therefore.**)

4. I won't have the book; **therefore,** I will use another book. (There are two separate sentences here, so you need a semicolon. You **cannot** use a comma instead of the semicolon; that would be a run-on sentence. Once again, you could use a period and make them two separate sentences.)

- -
Note: There are other ways to write the above sentences:

1. However, the book is not in the library.
1. The book, however, is not in the library.

2. I couldn't find the book, but I think the library has it.
2. Even though I couldn't find the book, I think the library has it.

3. Therefore, I won't have the book to help me.
3. I won't, therefore, have the book to help me.

4. I won't have the book, so I will use another book.
4. Because I won't have the book, I will use another book.

‑ ‑

58. *I/Me, He/Him, She/Her, Who/Whom*

This can be a tough one!

Here is the story . . .

There are these things called **cases** in the English language—and other languages too. Latin has five! English has only three, and we are going to concern ourselves with only two of them: **subjective case** and **objective case.** *Pronouns have case.* No other part of speech has case that concerns us. When the pronoun is the subject of the sentence (or a predicate nominative, a pronoun that follows a linking verb like *to be*), you use the subjective case. When the pronoun is a direct object, an indirect object, or the object of a preposition, you use the objective case. Really, it is as simple as that! Refer to Sections 9, 10, and 11 for information about subjects, predicate nominatives, and objects.

Subjective Case	**Objective Case**
I	me
we	us
he	him
she	her
they	them
who	whom

Examples: **I** went to the store. (**I** is the subject of the sentence.)

He and I went to the store. (Both pronouns are the subjects of the sentence.)

I gave **her** the money. (**I** is the subject, and **her** is the indirect object.)

I gave Sue and **her** the money. (**Sue** and **her** are both indirect objects.)

He gave **him** and **me** the money. (***Him*** and ***me*** are both indirect objects.)

He gave the money to **him** and **me**. (***Him*** and ***me*** are both objects of the preposition ***to.***)

Who is that man over there? (***Who*** is the subject.)

To **whom** did you give the money? (***Whom*** is the object of the preposition ***to.***)

Whom did you see? (Change the question to a statement and you get **You did see whom. *Whom*** is the direct object. ***You*** is the subject.)

Helpful Hints!

People seem to run into problems when there are two pronouns after a verb, or a name and a pronoun. For example: He saw **he** and **I** at the movies. You wouldn't say **He saw *he* at the movies,** would you? And you wouldn't say **He saw *I* at the movies.** Therefore, you wouldn't say **He saw *he and I* at the movies!** It should be **He saw *him and me* at the movies.**

Take one of the pronouns away and see if the other sounds right by itself.

Sometimes pronouns come after words like ***for, with, to,*** and ***from.*** Since these words are prepositions, the pronouns after them are objects of the preposition and are in objective case. For example: Please take a picture of **him and her.**

✓ 59. *Imply/Infer*

To ***imply*** is to suggest something without coming right out and saying it.

To ***infer*** is to conclude something from what has been said or suggested.

These two words are similar, but opposite. You can **imply** something; someone else will listen to you and **infer** something from what you said. Alternatively, someone may **imply** something by what they say; you will then **infer** something from what they said.

Examples: Jane **implied** that she would not be attending the party.

I **inferred** from her conversation that Jane is not attending the party.

60. Punctuation of Abbreviations

Many abbreviations do not have a period after them, for example, **ft** (foot), **mg** (milligram), **oz** (ounce), **lb** (pound), **gm** (gram), and **yd** (yard).

However, **in.** (inch) is followed by a period, so that it is not confused with the preposition **in.**

While we are talking about abbreviations, notice that many of those with all capital letters have no periods within them.

Examples: FBI, TV, CIA, USA, YMCA

Inc. (incorporated), **co.** (company), and **corp.** (corporation) are always followed by a period.

61. *Its/It's*

It's means **"it is."** It is a contraction.

Its is a possessive. It does not mean **"it is."**

Examples: **It's** raining today. (**It is** raining today.)

The dog ate its food. (The food belongs to the dog. **Its** is possessive here. It does not mean *"it is."*)

62. *This/Those* With *Kind* and *Type*

Kind and **type** are singular words. Use the singular pronoun **this** or **that** with them. However, if you say **types** or **kinds,** then use **these** or **those,** which are plural. The adjective and the noun must match: both singular or both plural.

Examples: **This type** of butterfly is usually spotted.

I have ***these types*** of coins in my collection. (Do not say **I have *these type* of coins in my collection.**)

63. *Lay/Lie*

Back in Section 3, we talked about verbs. You may want to look back there now to refresh your memory about transitive and intransitive verbs. Transitive verbs have a direct object; intransitive verbs do not.

The verb *lay* is transitive. It has a direct object.

The verb *lie* is intransitive. It does **not** have a direct object.

In other words, you must lay **something,** but you don't lie something.

Examples: I will **lay** my hat on the table. (Lay what? Hat. Hat is the direct object.)

She lies in the sun. (Lies what? Nothing. **Lies** has no direct object.)

She **is laying** a blanket on the bed. (Laying what? Blanket.)

The dog **is lying** on his back. (Lying what? **Lying** has no direct object.)

Part of the problem with these two verbs concerns the forms for the different tenses, which are quite confusing. Here are examples of the correct usage for each verb.

Lie	Lay
I **lie** down.	I **lay** my coat on the chair.
Yesterday, I **lay** down.	Yesterday, I **laid** my coat on the chair.
I have often **lain** down.	I have often **laid** my coat on the chair.

Part of the confusion is that the past tense of *lie* is *lay!* However, the past tense of *lay* is *laid!* No wonder we are all confused!

✓ 64. *Leave/Let*

Leave means to go away. **Let** means to allow.

Correct: **Leave** her alone for a while.

Let her go to the movies.

Incorrect:	**Let** her alone for a while.
	Leave her go to the movies.

65. Less/Fewer

The difference between **less** and **fewer** can be a tricky one. You might try to go by how it sounds, but there is really a simple rule. **Less** is used with singular words and tells how much. **Fewer** is used with plural words and tells how many.

Examples:	I use **less** salt when I cook than my mother did. (**Salt** is singular.)
	I planted **fewer** flowers this year than last. (**Flowers** is plural.)

66. Like/As if

Like is a preposition and introduces a phrase. **As** and **as if** are subordinating conjunctions and introduce clauses (see Section 13).

Examples:	She looks **like an angel.** (prepositional phrase)
	I studied hard for the test **as my teacher recommended.** (Do not say not **like my teacher recommended;** *as my teacher recommended* is a clause with the verb **recommended.**)
	It looks **as if it might rain today.** (Do not say **like it might rain;** *as if it might rain* is a clause with the verb **rain.**)

Helpful Hint! If there is a verb in what follows, don't use **like.**

---

67. Lose/Loose

Lose is a verb. **Loose** is an adjective. The **s** in **lose** sounds like a **z.**

Examples:　　I hope I don't **lose** my glasses again.

My pants are too **loose.**

68. *Only:* Where to Put It

Only is an adverb. You must be really careful about where you put it in the sentence because different placements of the word *only* change the meaning of a sentence. Check it out:

Examples:　　She **only** danced in the talent show. (She danced, but she didn't do anything else.)

She danced **only** in the talent show. (She didn't dance anywhere else.)

She danced in the **only** talent show. (There was no other talent show.)

Only she danced in the talent show. (No one else danced in the show.)

See what I mean?

69. *Percent*

Percent is one word and is used with a number.

Example:　　I spent about **50 percent** of my money.

70. *Principal/Principle*

The **principal** is the man or woman who runs the school—he or she is your "pal." *Principal* also means the **main one,** such as a **principal** actor. A **principle** is a rule or belief.

Examples:　　I had to go to the **principal's** office because I was talking too much in class.

He explained to me the **principles** of behaving in the classroom!

71. Titles: Italics or Quotes?

Quotes have other purposes in addition to setting off someone's exact words. They are used for certain titles. Italics are also used for some titles and have other uses as well. When you are writing by hand, you cannot do italics. You <u>underline</u> instead. When using a computer, use italics.

Generally speaking, **the whole thing is italicized; parts are quoted:**

Use Italics (or underline)	Use Quotes
Book titles	Short stories
Movie titles	Chapter titles
TV show titles	Title of one episode of a TV show
CD titles	Song titles
Magazine names	Article in a magazine
Operas	An aria in an opera
Poems that are book length	Short poem
Ship, airplane, and spacecraft names	

72. *Real* and *Really*

Real is an adjective; *really* is an adverb. Here are the proper usages:

> You look **really** nice today. (**Really** is an adverb modifying the adjective **nice.** It answers the question "**how** nice?")

> Are those **real** diamonds? (**Real** is an adjective modifying the noun **diamonds.**)

The words **very** and **really** can be overused. You can use these words instead: **especially, unusually, extremely, particularly, exceptionally, exceedingly,** or **incredibly.**

73. *Rise/Raise*

These two verbs are in the same category as **lie** and **lay** (Section 63).

The verb **raise** is transitive. It has a direct object.

The verb **rise** is intransitive. It does not have a direct object.

In other words, you must **raise** something, but you don't **rise** something.

Examples: I will **raise** the flag. (Raise what? Flag. *Flag* is the direct object.)

I usually **rise** at 6 a.m. (Rise what? Nothing. It has no direct object.)

Please **raise** your hand to ask a question. (Raise what? Hand.)

The sun is **rising**. (Rising what? Nothing. There is no direct object.)

Part of the confusion with these two verbs concerns the different tenses. Here are examples of correct usage of each verb:

Rise	Raise
I **rise** from the chair.	I will **raise** my hand in class.
Yesterday, I **rose** at dawn.	Yesterday, I **raised** the flag at school.
I have often **risen** too late.	I have often **raised** the flag at school.

74. Shall/Will

There is no need to use **shall.** If you really want to use it, here is the rule:

For future tense in formal writing, use **shall** only with first person (**I** or **we**). Use **will** with **you, he, they, she, who,** and **it.**

Example: I **shall** make a speech at the board meeting.

To indicate determination or threat, use **will** with **I** or **we,** but use **shall** with **you, he, she, they, it,** or **who.**

You **shall** clean your room!

I **will** win the marathon!

75. Sit/Set

These two verbs are in the same category as **lie/lay** and **rise/raise** (Sections 63 and 73).

The verb **set** is transitive. It has a direct object.

The verb **sit** is intransitive. It does not have a direct object.

In other words, you must **set** something, but you don't **sit** something.

Examples: I will **set** the book on the table. (Set what? Book. **Book** is the direct object.)

I **sit** in the chair (Sit what? Nothing. It has no direct object.)

Please **set** the bag on the table. (Set what? Bag.)

Sit in the chair. (Sit what? There is no direct object.)

Part of the problem with these two verbs concerns the different tenses, which can be confusing. Here are examples of correct usage of each verb.

Sit	**Set**
I **sit** in the chair.	I now **set** the box here.
Yesterday, I **sat** in the chair.	Yesterday, I **set** the box here.
I have often **sat** in the chair.	I have often **set** the box here.

76. Stationary/Stationery

The **stationary** with the **ary** means **stays in one place**. Think of the **a** in station**a**ry and the **a** in pl**a**ce.

The stationery with the **e** is the one on which you write.

77. Than/Then

Then is an adverb. It tells **when.**

Example: What did you do **then?**

- -
Note: It is important to know that **then** is NOT a conjunction and cannot join two sentences together! You need a conjunction to use with **then.**
- -

| Incorrect: | I ate dinner, **then** I went to the movies. (Run-on sentence) |
| Correct: | I ate dinner, **and then** I went to the movies. |

Don't get *then* confused with *than*. *Than* is used in comparisons. (See Section 85.)

| *Example:* | I am taller **than** he is. |

78. *That/Who/Which*

That, who, and *which* are relative pronouns; they are used to begin an adjective clause. *Who* is used for people, and *which* is used for things.

Examples:	The dress, **which** was on sale, is blue and white.
	Mr. Frank, **who** is my neighbor, is going to France next week.
	He is the boy **who** was in the accident.

That is generally used for things **in essential clauses;** those are the clauses without commas around them because you really cannot leave them out.

| *Example:* | This is the dress **that** I wore to the wedding. (*That I wore to the wedding* is necessary information about the dress. You wouldn't leave it out, you probably would not pause before and after saying it, and, therefore, you would not put commas around it.) |

79. *They're/Their/There*

They're is the contraction that means *they are.*

Their is a possessive pronoun that shows ownership.

There is an adverb that tells where.

Examples:	**They're** going to the movies today. (**They are** going to the movies today.)
	Their house is for sale. (The house belongs to them.)
	There is a cup on the table. I put it **there**.

80. *To/Too/Two*

Two is a number.

To is a preposition.

Too means *also.* It can also mean *very.*

> *Examples:* I have **two** pencils.
>
> I am going **to** school now.
>
> Are you going **too**? I, **too,** am going. It is **too** far to walk.

Note: When *too* means *also* (in the last example above), notice that you do *not* need a comma when *too* is at the end of the sentence. However, if *too* interrupts the sentence, it is set off with commas.

---

81. *Who's/Whose*

Who's means *who is.* It is a contraction. *Whose* is possessive.

> *Examples:* **Who's** coming to dinner? (**Who is** coming to dinner?)
>
> **Whose** book is this? (You wouldn't say **Who is** book is this? *Whose* implies ownership.)

82. *Cloths/Clothes*

Clothes are what you wear. *Cloths* are what you dust with. Enough said.

83. *Vice versa*

This means *and the other way around.* Most people know this, but sometimes they say *visa versa.* It is just *vice versa.*

Chapter 6

Some Grammar Issues

Don't use words too big for the subject.
Don't say "infinitely" when you mean "very";
otherwise you'll have no word left
when you want to talk about
something
really infinite.

C. S. Lewis
English essayist and novelist (1898–1963)

This chapter covers some ways to improve your writing and things to watch out for.

Chapter 6 Quiz:
How Much Do You Know
About These Grammar Issues?

Take this quiz before you read Chapter 6. The answers are on the back of this page.

Circle the correct answer in each sentence.

1. Everyone has (their, his or her) own pizza.

2. Neither John nor Jim (is, are) bringing a date.

3. The poodle is the (tallest, taller) of the two dogs.

4. The (children's, childrens') toys were all broken.

5. (Thomas', Thomas's) briefcase was stolen.

6. All the (boy's, boys) were tall.

7. Seven (girl's, girls') pies were in the contest.

8. I went to the zoo, and I (met, meet) my friend there.

9. I have (swum, swam) every day this week.

10. I (brought, brang) the phone back to the store.

11. I have (lain, laid) in the sun for an hour.

12. The dog (drug, dragged) a branch into the house.

Answers to Chapter 6 Quiz

1. Everyone has (their, **his or her**) own pizza.

2. Neither John nor Jim (**is,** are) bringing a date.

3. The poodle is the (tallest, **taller**) of the two dogs.

4. The (**children's,** childrens') toys were all broken.

5. (Thomas', **Thomas's**) briefcase was stolen.

6. All the (boy's, **boys**) were tall.

7. Several (girl's, **girls'**) pies were in the contest.

8. I went to the zoo, and I (**met,** meet) my friend there.

9. I have (**swum,** swam) every day this week.

10. I (**brought,** brang) the phone back to the store.

11. I have (**lain,** laid) in the sun for an hour.

12. The dog (drug, **dragged**) a branch into the house.

12 correct: Grammar Whiz!!
10–11 correct: Very Good!
8–9 correct: Pretty Good!
7 or fewer correct: Need Some Practice!

84. Agreement

By agreement we mean that singular subjects go with singular verbs, and a singular pronoun has a singular antecedent. (Remember that the antecedent is the word that the pronoun is standing in for.)

Example: **He is** a medical student. (**He** is a singular pronoun, and **is** is a singular verb form.)

How can you tell which verb form is singular? Try using the verb with **he** and **they.** The form of the verb that sounds right with **he** is singular, and the form of the verb that sounds right with **they** is plural.

Example: **He runs** three miles each day. **They run** three miles each day.

Runs is the singular verb form, and **run** is the plural verb form. (Notice that this is opposite of nouns, where the plural form has the **s** at the end.)

Pronoun and Verb Agreement

Most problems with agreement concern the indefinite pronouns such as **none, everyone, some, neither, either, anyone, someone, few, many, all,** etc. Most of these pronouns are singular. Some can be either singular or plural. (See Section 2 for more information about pronouns.)

Some singular indefinite pronouns: anybody, somebody, everybody, nobody, anything, everything, something, nothing, no one, everyone, someone, anyone, each, either, neither, nothing, one

Some plural indefinite pronouns: both, few, many, several

Pronouns that can be either: all, any, more, most, some, none

Examples of singular pronouns agreeing with singular verbs:

Everyone is going to the party.

Each of us **is** planning a vacation (not **are** planning).

Examples of plural pronouns agreeing with plural verbs:

>**Both are** fine with me.
>
>**Few** of us **are** going.

Examples of pronouns that can be either:

>**Most** of the cake **is** gone.
>
>**Most** of the people **are** going.
>
>The word in the prepositional phrase following the pronoun determines singular or plural (**cake** is singular; **people** is plural).

Pronoun and Antecedent Agreement

Once again, the problems are with those indefinite pronouns!

Examples: **Everyone** is bringing **his or her** friend. (Use **his or her** because it must agree with **everyone,** which is a singular pronoun even though it sounds as if it would be plural.)

Many are bringing **their** friends. (Use **their** because it must agree with **many,** which is plural.)

Either/Or and *Neither/Nor*

Rule 1:   Two words connected with **and** are always considered plural and take a plural pronoun.

Example: **John and James** took **their** dog for a walk. (Use **their** because it is plural and agrees with **John and James,** which is also plural.)

Rule 2:   Two words connected with **either/or** or **neither/nor** are singular if both of the words are singular.

Example: **Neither John nor James is** bringing **his** date to the party. (**Neither John nor James** is singular, so you use **is,** the singular verb, and **his,** the singular pronoun.)

Rule 3:   As if this isn't all confusing enough, when two words are connected with **either/or** or **neither/nor** and one is plural and one is singular, the one closest to the verb or pronoun agrees.

Examples: **Neither the boy nor the girls are** bringing **their** dates. (Since **girls** is plural and closer to the verb and pronoun than **boy,** use the plural verb **are bringing** and the plural pronoun **their.**)

Neither the girls nor the boy is bringing **his** date. (Since **boy** is singular and closest to the verb and pronoun, use the singular verb **is bringing** and the singular pronoun **his.**)

Collective Noun Agreement With Verb and Pronoun

Remember that a collective noun (see Section 1) is a singular noun that refers to a group, such as **family, band, club, class,** or **flock.** If the collective noun is referring to the group as a whole, it is considered singular and takes a singular verb and pronoun. If the collective noun refers to each member of the group separately, it is considered plural and takes a plural verb and pronoun. This can sometimes be difficult to figure out.

Examples: My **family is** taking a trip this summer. (Since the whole family is going together, **family** is considered singular, and we use the singular verb **is.**)

My **family are** going to different places for Thanksgiving this year. (Since everyone is going to a different place, we are referring to the members of the family separately, and we use the plural verb form **are.**)

The **band is** marching in the parade. (They are all marching together.)

The **band are** tuning their instruments. (We assume that each member is tuning his or her particular instrument separately.)

85. Comparison

Comparison involves adjectives and adverbs.

Examples: I am **tall.**

My brother is **taller** than I am. (The **-er** form is called **comparative** and is used to compare two things or people.)

My sister is the **tallest** of all of us. (The **-est** form is called **superlative** and is used to compare more than two things or people).

Some adjectives do not have **-er** and **-est** forms. For example, there is no such word as **funner** or **funnest**. (Please do not use them!) With these words, you use **more** and **most** in front of them.

Note: Do not use **more** or **most** with **-er** or **-est!**

Do not say **This room is more cleaner than that one.**

Do say **This room is cleaner than that one.**

Examples: Tennis is **more fun** than golf.

Surfing is the **most fun** of all three sports!

Adverbs do not have **-er** and **-est** forms. With adverbs, use **more** and **most.**

Examples: She sang **quietly.**

He sang **more quietly** than she did.

I sang the **most quietly** of all.

Helpful Hint! Watch out for "faulty comparison."

Examples: **She likes pizza more than me.**

Does that mean that she likes pizza more than I like pizza, **or** does it mean she likes pizza more than she likes me? Well, it most likely means she likes pizza more than I like pizza, so say it correctly:

She likes pizza more than I do.

---

86. Dangling and Misplaced Modifiers

Take a look at these sentences:

1. While still in diapers, my mother graduated from college.

2. The poet read from his new book wearing glasses.

3. Growling, I fed my hungry dog.

4. The girl walked her dog in a bikini.

The above sentences should make you laugh. The mistakes are common and easy to make, but the sentences come out either unclear or downright ridiculous!

1. The first sentence **says** that **my mother graduated from college while she was still in diapers.** Obviously, this is not what the writer intended; my mother graduated from college while **I** was still in diapers. However, the word **mother** is placed right next to **while still in diapers.** When words are next to each other, it is assumed that they go with each other.

Correct: My mother graduated from college while I was still in diapers.   OR

While I was still in diapers, my mother graduated from college.

2. Was the poet wearing glasses, or was the book wearing glasses? The sentence says that the new book was wearing glasses, but we know that is not the case. Make the sentence clearer. Put the **wearing glasses** phrase next to who was really wearing glasses!

Correct:	Wearing glasses, the poet read from his book. OR
	The poet wore glasses while he read from his book.
	(There are usually several ways to correct a sentence, so there are other options for fixing this sentence.)

3. Who was growling? Obviously, it was the dog. However, this sentence says that **I** was growling.

Correct:	Because he was growling, I fed my hungry dog. OR
	I fed my hungry, growling dog.

4. Who was wearing the bikini? Well, sometimes dogs do wear fancy outfits, but it was most likely the girl who was wearing the bikini!

Correct:	The girl wearing the bikini was walking her dog. OR
	The girl, wearing a bikini, was walking her dog. OR
	While wearing a bikini, the girl was walking her dog.

87. Possessives

Possessives show ownership. Only nouns and pronouns can be possessive. Generally, to form a possessive noun add an **apostrophe** and an *s.*

Examples:	**Sarah's** ball fell behind the sofa.
	The **boy's** toy is lost.

To make a plural noun that ends in **s** possessive, you usually just add an apostrophe after the **s.**

Examples:	The **boys'** toys were lost. (More than one boy's toys were lost.)
	The **houses'** lights were all off. (More than one house has the lights off.)

When a plural does not end in **s,** add an **apostrophe** and an **s** for the possessive.

> ***Example:*** The children's toys were all broken. (***Children*** is already plural without an **s.**)

Sometimes, a **singular** word that ends in **s** will have an **apostrophe** and an **s** added to make it possessive.

> ***Example:*** **James's** essay was very good. (The two **s**'s in a row might look odd, but notice how you pronounce **James's;** you pronounce it just the way it is spelled. You do not pronounce it **James'.**)

Think about how you would say the word when deciding whether to add an **apostrophe** and an **s** to a word that already has an **s** at the end. For example, ***princesses*** is a plural word. To make it possessive, you would simply add an **apostrophe.** You would not say ***princesses's*** gowns. You would say ***princesses'*** gowns (the same way you would pronounce the plural ***princesses***). For the singular possessive you would write (and say) ***princess's.*** Actually, the singular and plural possessives would be pronounced the same, although spelled differently (***princess's*** and ***princesses'.***)

Helpful Hint! Do not EVER use an apostrophe to make a noun plural! The plural of **boy** is **boys,** not **boy's** (**boy's** is possessive). That goes for all nouns! The only time you use an apostrophe to make a word plural is for letters (**a**'s), numbers (**4**'s), symbols (**&**'s), and words used as themselves (for example: You have too many *and*'s in that sentence). Although a word used as itself is *italicized,* the **apostrophe** and the **s** are not. (In this book, I have used **bold italics** for words used as themselves, but in usual text, words used as themselves are simply italicized.)

Another Helpful Hint! Possessive pronouns do not have apostrophes.

> ***Examples:*** The book is **ours.** The toy is **theirs.** This dress is **yours.** I know **its** name. **Whose** book is that?

---

88. Active and Passive Voices

We talked a little about active and passive voice back in Section 2 (Verbs).

To review, in **active voice** the subject in the sentence is the thing or person doing the action of the verb. In **passive voice** the verb is being done by someone or something other than the subject (the doer of the verb in passive voice may or may not be mentioned in the sentence).

Examples of active voice:

> **I am swimming** today.

> **The boy drove** the car to school today.

> **The dogs ran** away yesterday.

Examples of passive voice:

> **The boy was driven** to school. (The **boy** is the subject, but he did not do the driving.)

> **The school was built** in the 1900's. (The **school** is the subject, but it didn't build anything.)

Helpful Hint! The lesson here is to use the **active voice** most of the time in your writing. It is much stronger. Use the **passive voice** if

> You don't know who did it (**The fire was set** in the bathroom.)

> You don't really care who did it. (**Audrey was awarded** the gold medal.) The focus here is on Audrey getting the medal, not who gave it to her.

---

89. Using Strong Verbs

Your writing will be more lively and to the point if you choose your verbs carefully. With active verbs, you need fewer adverbs. The most important thing to remember is to not overuse the verb *to be.* The forms of *to be* include the following: *are, is, have been, am, was.*

Not so great:	There will be a meeting of the dance committee on Friday.
Better:	The dance committee will meet on Friday (shorter and more to the point).
Not so great:	It is really nice out today.
Better:	The sun is shining today (more descriptive)!

- -

Note: Remember that forms of the **to be** verb are often used as helping verbs with a main verb. It is fine to use those verbs (such as **are, am, will be, has been,** etc.) as helping verbs with another verb (for example, **is shining,** in the example above).

- -

Helpful Hint! Avoid using **there is** (or **there was,** or **there will be,** etc.) to begin a sentence. It is very weak.

90. Verb Tense Consistency

The 12 verb tenses were discussed in Section 3. Avoid mixing tenses needlessly. Stay consistent!

Not this:	I **went** to her house, and she **gives** me some cookies (needless switch from present to past tense).
Do this:	I **went** to her house, and she **gave** me some cookies.

If you begin telling a story in past tense, don't suddenly switch to present tense. Things that happen at the same time should be expressed in the same tense.

91. Irregular Verb Forms

An irregular verb is a verb that does not add **-ed** or **-d** to make it past tense. The problem is that the English language has tons of irregular verbs that just need to be memorized. Here is a regular verb:

I walk	**I walked**	**I have walked**

Here are some common problematic irregular verb forms:

I swim	Yesterday, I swam	Every day, I have swum
I ring	Yesterday, I rang	Every day, I have rung
I swing	Yesterday, I swung	Every day, I have swung
I shrink	Yesterday, I shrank	Every day, I have shrunk
I drink	Yesterday, I drank	Every day, I have drunk
I bring	Yesterday, I brought	Every day, I have brought
It costs	Yesterday, it cost	Every day, it has cost
It bursts	Yesterday, it burst	Every day, it has burst
I lend	Yesterday, I lent	Every day, I have lent
I lead	Yesterday, I led	Every day, I have led
I wear	Yesterday, I wore	Every day, I have worn
I write	Yesterday, I wrote	Every day, I have written
I run	Yesterday, I ran	Every day, I have run
I throw	Yesterday, I threw	Every day, I have thrown
I speak	Yesterday, I spoke	Every day, I have spoken
I wake	Yesterday, I woke	Every day, I have woken
I lie	Yesterday, I lay	Every day, I have lain
I lay	Yesterday, I laid	Every day, I have laid
I sit	Yesterday, I sat	Every day, I have sat

I set	Yesterday, I set	Every day, I have set
I rise	Yesterday, I rose	Every day, I have risen
I bought	Yesterday, I bought	Every day, I have bought
I drag	Yesterday, I dragged	Every day, I have dragged

Helpful Hint! Please note that **brang** and **broughten** are not words; as weird as it sounds, **I have swum** and **I have drunk** are indeed correct; **I have went** should be **I have gone;** and you may **have hanged** a man, but you have **hung** curtains! Since it is a regular verb, **sneak** becomes **sneaked,** not **snuck!**

---

92. Linking/Action Verbs With Pronouns

Just a little review here . . .

In Section 3 we discussed verbs, in Section 11 we discussed predicate words, and then in Section 58, we talked about when to use **I** and when to use **me.** When you use a linking verb, as opposed to an action verb, you use the subjective pronoun forms **I, he, she, they, we,** or **who** after the verb (rather than **me, him, her, them, us,** or **whom**). The pronoun after the linking verb is a **predicate nominative** and in the subjective case.

Therefore, as weird as it sounds, **It is I** is correct, not **It is me.**

93. Parallel Structure

Parallel structure is the repetition of a grammatical pattern in a sentence. It is best understood by example.

Not Parallel: I like to swim, to ski, and hunting.

Parallel: I like to swim, to ski, and to hunt.

Not parallel: He is kind, honest, and a good student. (***Kind*** and ***honest*** are adjectives, so ***a good student*** should be made into an adjective; you can also make ***kind*** and ***honest*** parallel with ***a good student.***)

Parallel: He is kind, honest, and conscientious.

Parallel: He is a kind boy, an honest citizen, and a good student.

Always use parallel structure.

Parallel structure is very important in lists. Here is an example:

Not Parallel: This book explains

- How to power up your computer.
- How to begin the program.
- Using the printer.

Parallel: This book explains

- How to power up your computer.
- How to begin the program.
- How to use the printer.

Make sure you use parallel form in an ***either/or*** or ***neither/nor*** construction too.

Not parallel: He is neither athletic nor likes music.

Parallel: He is neither athletic nor musical.

94. Verbals: Participles and Gerunds

We talked about **participles** and **participial phrases** in Section 12. Let's review them here and also discuss **gerunds,** which are similar.

Participles are verbs that are used as **adjectives.** They are usually in either the past tense form or the **-ing** form.

Examples: The **smiling** boy took a cookie. (***Smiling*** is usually a verb; here, however, it is an adjective describing ***boy.***)

The **fallen** snow looked beautiful. (***Fallen*** is a past tense of the verb ***fall,*** but here it is an adjective describing the snow.)

Gerunds are verbs that are used as **nouns.** Therefore, a gerund can be a subject or an object in a sentence. A gerund appears in the ***-ing*** form of the verb.

Examples: **Swimming** is my favorite hobby. (***Swim*** is usually a verb, but here it is a noun and the subject of the sentence.)

I like **running** in the snow. (***Running*** is usually a verb, but here it is a noun and the direct object of ***like.***)

Chapter 7

Finishing Touches

Let thy speech be short,
comprehending much in a few words.

Aprocrypha

This chapter contains more important ways to write better—and the grand finale: writing!

Chapter 7 Quiz:
How Much Do You Know
About These Finishing Touches?

Take this quiz before you read Chapter 7. The answers are on the back of this page.

1. How many words should be capitalized in this book title?
   and the winner is me!
   a. 3   b. 4   c. 5   d. 2

2. How many words should be capitalized in this book title?
   she was lost, but now she's found
   a. 6   b. 5   c. 7   d. 4

3. Which sentence is correct?   a   or   b
   a. I have 4 pens and 5 pencils.
   b. I have four pens and five pencils.

Circle the correct spelling:

4. acommodate	accomodate	accommodate
5. calendar	calender	callendar
6. embarrass	embarass	embarrase
7. existance	existence	existense
8. license	lisence	licence
9. milennium	millenium	millennium
10. mispell	misspell	miss-spell
11. occurance	occurence	occurrence
12. questionaire	questionnaire	questionnairre
13. recommend	reccommend	reccomend
14. referance	refference	reference
15. rhythm	rythym	rythm

Answers to Chapter 7 Quiz

1. How many words should be capitalized in this book title?
   And the Winner Is Me!
   a. 3   **b. 4**   c. 5   d. 2

2. How many words should be capitalized in this book title?
   She Was Lost, but Now She's Found
   (The answer could also be **c**; if all the words in the title are capitalized
   except one, you may go ahead and capitalize all of them.)
   a. 6   b. 5   c. 7   d. 4

3. Which sentence is correct?   a   or   **b**
   a) I have 4 pens and 5 pencils.
   b) I have four pens and five pencils.

Circle the correct spelling:

4. acommodate	accomodate	**accommodate**
5. **calendar**	calender	callendar
6. **embarrass**	embarass	embarrase
7. existance	**existence**	existense
8. **license**	lisence	licence
9. milennium	millenium	**millennium**
10. mispell	**misspell**	miss-spell
11. occurance	occurence	**occurrence**
12. questionaire	**questionnaire**	questionnairre
13. **recommend**	reccommend	reccomend
14. referance	refference	**reference**
15. **rhythm**	rythym	rythm

15 correct: Grammar Whiz!!
13–14 correct: Very Good!
11–12 correct: Pretty Good!
10 or fewer correct: Need Some Practice!

95. Capitalization in Titles

Here are the rules for capitalizing words in titles (book titles, movie titles, short story titles, song titles, chapter titles, etc.).

1. **Always** capitalize the first and last words of a title no matter what they are.

2. Capitalize both parts of any hyphenated words.

3. **Do not capitalize the following words unless they are the first or last word of a title:**

> Do not capitalize the articles ***a, an,*** or ***the***
>
> Do not capitalize the FANBOYS conjunctions (***for, and, nor, but, or, yet,*** and ***so***). However, if ***yet*** or ***so*** is being used as an adverb, do capitalize it!

4. Do not capitalize prepositions unless they are longer than three letters. (Do not capitalize short prepositions such as ***at, in, out, for, up, to;*** but do capitalize longer prepositions such as ***with, above, below, between, among.***) If the preposition has no phrase, it is not a preposition but an adverb, and it should be capitalized.

Helpful Hint! Remember that although it is short, the word ***is*** is a verb and should always be capitalized in a title!

Examples: Let's assume these are book titles:

> *So Near Yet So Far Away* (***So*** is an adverb here; ***yet*** is a conjunction but looks funny as the only lowercase [not capitalized] word in the title, so I would capitalize it here.)
>
> *I Am Going Out Tonight* (Although ***out*** can be a preposition, here it is not part of a prepositional phrase, for example, ***out the door***, so it is being used as an adverb and should be capitalized.)
>
> *What Is Going On?* (***Is*** is a verb and is always capitalized in a title.)

96. Series and Lists

If you have a series in a sentence, remember to use a comma after every item in the series, including the next to the last one (before **and**).

Use a colon to introduce a series in a sentence when the sentence ends before the series begins.

> **Example:**   I have these items in my purse: comb, pen, wallet, and keys. (There is a complete sentence before the series. The series does not complete the sentence.)

Do not use a colon to introduce a series in a sentence when the items are the ending part of the sentence.

> **Example:**   In my purse I have a comb, a pen, a wallet, and keys. (You would not put a colon after **have** because it would cut the sentence in half.)

Note that the words *follow* or *following* often, but not always, precede a list.

For vertical lists, use a colon after the introductory sentence. You do not need to capitalize the items in the list (unless they are complete sentences, in which case you would begin each one with a capital letter).

> **Examples:**   I have the following items in my wallet:
>
> - pen
> - comb
> - wallet
> - keys
>
> Make sure you do the following tasks:
> - Clean the kitchen.
> - Water the plants.
> - Vacuum the rugs.
> - Get the mail.

If the items in the list complete the introductory sentence, do not use a colon.

Example: In my purse I have

- a pen
- a comb
- a wallet
- keys

97. Keep It Simple

When a journalist writes a newspaper article, it needs to fit in the allotted space, so the editor will sometimes chop out the unnecessary words. Much of what we write is too wordy and can be slimmed down. Do not think that using big words and using lots of them improves your writing. It makes it more difficult to understand. Your writing goal (and speaking goal) is to be easily understood.

Wordy: He is a man who is very successful.

Better: He is successful.

Wordy: There will be a meeting held in the auditorium by the dance committee on Friday morning.

Better: The dance committee will meet in the auditorium Friday morning.

98. Numbers: When to Spell Them Out

In general spell out numbers up through ten in text. Use numerals (for example, *15*) for anything above ten. However, in literary writing, or when writing something scholarly in the humanities, numbers through ninety-nine are spelled out. Note that numbers from twenty-one through ninety-nine are hyphenated when they are two words.

If you have a sentence with two related numbers and one is over ten and one under, treat them the same way.

Example: The class consisted of **8 boys** and **16 girls.**

Never begin a sentence with a numeral.

> **Example:** **Sixty boys** were waiting in line. (You cannot use **60** here.)

Always use numerals in tables and charts.

Instead of a series of zeroes, you can spell out numbers such as **three million.**

Dimensions, sizes, and exact temperatures are always expressed in numerals. For example, **She wears a size 12 dress.**

With **a.m.** or **p.m.** always use numbers.

With **o'clock** you can use either words or numbers.

Fractions such as **two-thirds** are hyphenated.

99. Commonly Misspelled Words

These words are common—and commonly misspelled:

Accidentally	Accommodate
Acquire	Believe
Calendar	Category
Cemetery	Changeable
Column	Committed
Conscience (the guilty kind)	Conscientious
Conscious (or unconscious!)	Definitely
Discipline	Embarrass
Existence	Foreign
Gauge	Guarantee
Harass	Humorous
Immediately	Inoculate

Intelligence	Jewelry
Judgment	Kernel (corn) (*Colonel* is the military rank.)
Leisure	Liaison
Library	License
Maintenance	Millennium
Minuscule	Mischievous
Misspell	Noticeable
Occasionally	Occurrence
Perseverance	Possession
Precede (to come before something else)	Proceed (to go ahead)
Privilege	Pronunciation
Questionnaire	Receive/Receipt
Recommend	Referred
Reference	Relevant
Restaurant	Rhyme
Rhythm	Schedule
Separate	Twelfth
Until	Vacuum
Weird	

100. Commonly Mispronounced Words

The following words are commonly mispronounced:

Acrost—should be **across** (no *t* at the end)

Supposably—should be suppo**sed**ly

Undoubtably—should be undoub**ted**ly

Heighth—should be height (with a **t** sound at the end, not **th**)

Jewlery—should be je**wel**ry

Liberry—should be library (don't forget the **r**)

Febyuary—should be February (don't forget the **r**)

Mischeevious—should be mischievous with the accent on the first syllable and the last syllable having a **vus** sound.

Perscription—should be **pre**scription

Probly—should be pro**bab**ly

Pronounciation—should be pro**nun**ciation

Realator—should be **real**tor

Reoccur—should be re**cur**

101. The Big Kahuna: Writing!!!

Now that you know all the rules as well as what you should avoid, it is time to write. After all, that is the whole point. Learning the rules doesn't do much good unless you apply them in your writing and speaking.

Above all, writing should be clear and easy to understand. We are not talking about writing the Great American Novel here. We are talking about things you might write at your job or at school, such as memos, letters, and reports.

You don't need to use big words, and you don't need to use large amounts of words to write well. However, your writing needs to be clear, well organized, and interesting. You can make your writing interesting by using descriptive verbs and a variety of sentence structures.

Paragraphs

A paragraph is made up of several sentences that are related. Letters, reports, and essays are usually made up of several paragraphs, but sometimes you might be writing just one paragraph—for a memo perhaps. A paragraph should have an introductory sentence, called a **topic sentence.** It introduces your topic for the paragraph; all the other sentences in the paragraph hang on that topic sentence and should be about the same topic. If you are writing just one paragraph, your paragraph should also have a concluding sentence to wrap things up. Within your paragraphs, use transition words (**to begin, next, finally,** etc.), if necessary, to make your writing flow.

Here is a sample memo, written as one paragraph:

The planning committee will hold a meeting on Thursday at 9 a.m. in the main conference room on the first floor. Committee members should be prepared to discuss several issues at this meeting. We will begin with a review of the new building plans. Please bring your blueprints if you have them. Next, we will talk about the budget for the new construction. We will be presenting our new, proposed budget. Finally, we would like to hear your opinions about the new recreation center on the 9th floor. We will be distributing a survey for your thoughts. Please bring your survey to the meeting. We look forward to what we hope will be a productive morning!

In the above memo, there is an opening, or topic sentence. The rest of the paragraph sticks to that topic (the meeting). The last sentence wraps it all up. The transition words **begin, next,** and **finally** are used to create flow from one idea to the next.

- -
Note: In this book I have not indented paragraphs. Instead, I have left a blank line between paragraphs. Either way is okay. However, if you are writing a school paper, find out which method is preferred. It is usually fine to leave the blank line between paragraphs in a business letter. If you leave blank lines, do not indent.
- -

Multi-Paragraph Writing

Whether you are writing an essay, a report, or a business letter, anything with multiple paragraphs follows a pattern: The opening paragraph, the introduction, tells the readers what you are going to tell them. The middle paragraph or paragraphs gives the readers the bulk of the information. The final paragraph, or conclusion, tells the readers what you just told them—and sometimes calls for some action to be taken.

The middle paragraphs are similar to the paragraphs we talked about in the previous section, when we discussed the structure of a paragraph. Each paragraph in a multi-paragraph writing (except the introduction and the conclusion) has a topic sentence, which tells what the paragraph is about. Every sentence in the paragraph sticks to that topic.

Here is an example of a multi-paragraph letter. It is a letter of complaint by a consumer who recently purchased a new refrigerator.

To Whom It May Concern:

Last month I purchased a refrigerator manufactured by your company. I bought it at ABC Appliance in Wonderville. The model number is 76400-3. I am writing to you at this time because I am very unhappy with the product for a couple of reasons. I am hoping you can do something to solve the problem.

To begin, immediately after the refrigerator was installed, it began making loud banging noises almost constantly. I called the repair number, and a repair person from your company took a look at it. Since it is under warrantee, there was no charge to me for this service. I did not think it was the icemaker making that noise, and the repair person assured me that it wasn't. He made some adjustments and told me the problem was fixed. Several hours later the banging noise began again. I have repeatedly called ABC Appliance, but they told me to call you.

In addition to the noise problem, the refrigerator does not keep food cool at a consistent temperature. Sometimes we find that our food has frozen in the refrigerator! Other times the food is hardly cold. All the members of my family have noticed this problem at different times.

Needless to say, I am very disappointed in the performance of this appliance. I do not have the confidence that it can be repaired. I would like to return the unit to the store for a full refund and buy another brand. I am hoping your company will authorize this refund. I believe my refrigerator is defective, but at the time do not trust the brand enough to buy a similar refrigerator.

Sincerely yours,
Joseph Smith

Glossary

Abstract noun   A noun that you cannot see, hear, touch, taste, or smell. Examples: happiness, thought

Active voice   Writing in which the subject of the sentence is performing the action of the verb. Example: She drove the car.

Adjective   One of the eight parts of speech. An adjective describes a noun or another adjective and usually tells what kind or how many. Examples: purple, pretty

Adverb   One of the eight parts of speech. An adverb describes a verb, an adjective, or another adverb and usually tells how, when, or to what extent. Examples: slowly, very, now

Agreement   The rule that singular subjects go with singular verbs, plural subjects go with plural verbs, singular pronouns go with singular antecedents, and plural pronouns go with plural antecedents. Examples: **Jim** always **has his** dog with **him** (singular). The **boys are playing** soccer with **their** dads (plural).

Antecedent   A pronoun stands in for a noun. That noun is called its antecedent. Example: **Mary** brought **her** book (***her*** refers to its antecedent, ***Mary***).

Appositive   A phrase that adds more information to a noun or pronoun. Example: Ben, **my older brother,** is twelve years old.

Article   The words ***a, an,*** and ***the.*** They are adjectives.

Clause   A group of words that has a subject and a verb. Example: That book, **which I read last night,** is a mystery.

Collective noun   A noun that even in its singular form represents a group. Examples: group, flock, bunch, herd

Common noun   A person, place, or thing that does not begin with a capital letter. Examples: boy, dog, house, radio

Comparative   The adjective or adverb form that is used when comparing two things, generally the *-er* or *more* form. Examples: **taller** of the two girls, **more fun** than the other game

Complex sentence   A sentence with one or more dependent clauses and one independent clause. Example: Although I am tired (dependent), I will go with you (independent).

Compound sentence   A sentence with two or more independent clauses. Example: **I am tired, but I will go with you.**

Compound-complex sentence   A sentence with one or more dependent clauses and two or more independent clauses. Example: Although I am tired (dependent), I will go with you (independent) and I will have fun (independent)!

Concrete noun   A person, place, or thing you can see, hear, feel, taste, and/or smell. Examples: desk, teacher, computer

Dash (– en, — em)   The en dash is used for ranges of numbers and minus signs. The em dash is used for a break in thought in a sentence.

Demonstrative pronoun   The pronouns that are used to point out: *this, that, these,* and *those*

Direct object   A noun or pronoun that generally comes after the verb and receives its action. Example: I threw the **ball.**

Double negative   The use of two negatives, which makes it a positive and is grammatically incorrect. Examples: I **don't** have **no** paper. I am **not hardly** ready.

Fragment   A group of words that is intended to be a sentence, but instead is an incomplete thought. Example: Because I said so.

Gerund   A verb form ending in *-ing* that is used as a noun rather than a verb. Example: **Reading** is my favorite hobby.

Indefinite pronoun   Pronouns such as *anyone, anything, anybody, everyone, everything, everybody, someone, something, someone, none, few,* and *all.* Most, but not all, of these pronouns are singular.

Independent clause   A sentence (or complete thought)

Indirect object   Noun or pronoun that *receives* the direct object in a sentence. Example: He gave **me** the map.

Infinitive   A verb preceded by the word *to.* Example: to run

Intensive pronoun   A pronoun that ends in *-self* or *-selves.* Reflexive pronouns have the same form but a slightly different use. Example: I myself baked that beautiful cake!

Interjection   One of the eight parts of speech: a word that expresses emotion. Example: ouch! wow! oh!

Interrogative pronoun   The pronouns that are used to ask questions: *which, who, whom, whose,* and *what*

Irregular verb   A verb that does not form its past tense with the addition of *-ed.* Examples: **run** (ran), **see** (saw), **sit** (sat)

Italics   *Tilted letters in print.* You cannot write by hand in italics.

Linking verb   A verb that functions as an equal sign in a sentence, where both sides of the verb are equal. The most common linking verb is *to be* (*am, are, is*). Example: He **is** a boy.

Lowercase   Another word for small letters, as opposed to capital letters (uppercase).

Noun   One of the eight parts of speech: a person, place, thing, or idea. Examples: car, dog, city, sofa, thought

Objective case   The pronoun forms that are used as direct and indirect objects, and objects of a preposition. They are *me, us, her, him, them,* and *whom.*

Participle   A verb form, usually the past tense or *-ing* form that is used as an adjective. Example: I drove past the **burning** building.

Passive voice   Grammatical construction where the subject of the sentence is not performing the action of the verb. Example: I was driven to school.

Phrase   A small group of related words that does not contain both a subject and a verb. Examples: in the sun, jumping constantly, my next-door neighbor

Possessive   A form of a noun or pronoun that shows ownership. Examples: hers, Susan's, the children's

Predicate   The simple predicate is the verb in the sentence. The complete predicate is the entire sentence except the subject.

Preposition   One of the eight parts of speech. A preposition is always the first word in a prepositional phrase. The phrase usually tells where or when. Examples: **in** the box, **after** the party

Pronoun   One of the eight parts of speech. A pronoun takes the place of a noun. Examples: She, this, who, someone, I

Proper noun   A noun that names a particular person, place, thing, or idea and begins with a capital letter. Examples: John, Texas, Pacific Ocean, Buddhism

Punctuation marks   The symbols that make text readable by telling the reader when to stop or pause. Examples: periods, commas, colons, semicolons, quotation marks, dashes, hyphens, parentheses

Reflexive pronoun   A pronoun that ends in *-self* or *-selves.* Intensive pronouns have the same form, but a slightly different usage. Example: I made this beautiful cake myself.

Relative pronoun   A pronoun that begins an adjective clause. They are *that, which, who, whom,* and *whose.* Examples: This is the dress **that** I just bought. My neighbor, **who** lives next door, is from Italy.

Run-on sentence   Two sentences (complete thoughts) with either no punctuation or a comma separating them. There needs to be either a period or semicolon separating them, or a conjunction added after the comma. Example: The flower is pink, it is very pretty.

Simple sentence   A sentence that consists of just one independent clause. Example: Jack and I went to the movies.

Subject   Noun or pronoun that the sentence is about. The subject generally performs the action of the verb. Examples: **She** saw the art exhibit. The **dog** bit the young child.

Subordinate clause (dependent)   A clause (group of words with a subject and a verb) that is not a complete thought and cannot stand alone as a sentence. Example: although I received my driver's license

Superlative The adjective or adverb form that is used when comparing more than two things, generally the *-est* or *most* form. Examples: **tallest** of all the girls, the **most fun** of the three games

Tense Form of a verb that tells when the action was done. The most common tenses are past, present, and future. Examples: I walk, I walked, I will walk

Uppercase Another word for capital letters, as opposed to small letters (lowercase).

Verb One of the eight parts of speech. Every sentence needs at least one verb. Represents action or a *state of being*. Examples: run, talk, cook, is, looks

Voice Active or passive. Tells whether the subject performs the action of the verb or not. Examples: She baked a cake (active voice). A cake was baked by her (passive voice).

Index

bigwords101
contact information

Check out the website at
www.bigwords101.com

Questions or comments??
E-mail us at **bigwords101@yahoo.com**

For information about *Best LITTLE Grammar Book*
seminars, book signings, or workshops,
please e-mail us.

The Best LITTLE Grammar Book Ever!
is available for purchase at
www.bigwords101.com,
online booksellers,
and by order at your favorite bookstore.

bigwords101
PO Box 4483
Petaluma, CA 94955

Made in the USA
Lexington, KY
10 June 2012